GH01057599

Syaney

Berlitz Publishing Company, Inc.
Princeton   Mexico City   Dublin   Eschborn   Singapore

Text:	Revised by Peter Needham; original text by Ken Bernstein
Editor:	Christopher Billy
Photography:	Jon Davison: pages 3, 4, 6, 8, 11,12, 14, 16, 18, 21, 26, 29, 30, 33, 35, 38, 41, 42, 45, 46, 49, 62, 66, 81, 82, 85, 86, 90, 94, 96, 100-101; Australian Tourist Commission: pages 50, 53, 54, 72.
Photo Editor:	Naomi Zinn
Layout:	Media Content Marketing, Inc.
Cartography:	Ortelius Design

ISBN 2-8315-6373-9
Revised 1999 – Second Printing April 2000

Printed in Switzerland
020/004 RP

CONTENTS

• A () in the text denotes a highly recommended sight

Sydney

SYDNEY AND THE SYDNEYSIDERS

Sunny, surf-fringed Sydney—gateway to Australia for most visitors—seems custom-built for outdoor enjoyment. Bold, bright, and alluring, the city glows with instant physical appeal. Airline passengers arriving at dawn (the time when many international flights touch down at Sydney International Airport) enjoy views of mists lifting slowly from grey-green, eucalyptus-filled valleys. Forested landscapes give way to terracotta roofs and glittering swimming pools as Australia's biggest and most cosmopolitan city unfolds below you. And if you fly in later in the day, the lights from the city skyline, as well as Sydney's beaches, and its yachts bobbing in the bottle-green sea are displayed to full advantage.

The city's glorious harbor, stretching about 20 km (12.4 miles) inland from the Pacific Ocean to the east, is its dominant feature, but the metropolis sprawls more than 60 km (37 miles) farther west toward the Blue Mountains. To the north and south of the city limits Sydney is bordered by two vast national parks.

Four million people—nearly a fifth of Australia's population—choose to live here, and you can see why. If the world had a lifestyle capital, Sydney would be a strong contender (which is richly ironic considering it started out as a British penal colony). The city is sun-drenched, sassy, energetic, fun-loving, and intensely outdoor-oriented. It is regularly ranked as one of the world's favorite tourist destinations; its residents know this and they revel in it.

Sydney's air and water are clean by international standards, the streets are safe, dining is varied and inexpensive, the people are chatty, and their love of leisure pursuits is legendary. Sydney's climate is pleasant and temperate, seldom falling

Life's a beach: in this case, Sydney's Bondi Beach, Australia's most famous stretch of sand.

below 10° C (50° F) in winter, with an average summer maximum of about 25° C (77° F).

Sydney Harbour, officially called Port Jackson, divides the city into north and south, with the great gray Harbour Bridge (completed in 1932) spanning the divide. Believe it or not, the stone towers (pylons) at either end of the bridge don't serve any structural purpose—they were built purely to prevent the structure from looking like a coathanger. Most of Sydney's activities and points of interest lie south of the bridge, including the Opera House, the city commercial center (known as "the CBD" for Central Business District), Darling Harbour, the historic Rocks district, Bondi Beach, raunchy Kings Cross, Woolloomooloo, trendy Paddington and innumerable corner shops and pubs.

The landscapes north of the bridge are leafy, suburban, and affluent, dotted with smaller commercial centers and offering excellent views from Taronga Zoo, outdoor dining on the Lower North Shore, and some lovely beaches further north.

On the harbor's south side, the area known as the Rocks, one of Sydney's oldest precincts, is chockablock with opportunities for browsing, strolling, eating, and drinking. Paddington Market is brimming with local talent on Saturdays. And Chinatown offers cheap eats, as does Leichhardt, Sydney's Italian quarter.

In such surroundings, Sydneysiders (as the city's residents are known) delight in outdoor activities, playing or watching cricket (the dominant summer sport) and rugby (the main winter sport). Other leading diversions include Australian Rules football, horseracing, swimming, yachting, or just lazing on the beach.

If you enjoy beach life, Sydney is for you. The city has about 70 beaches and they welcome all visitors; none is private. Beaches occupy a special position in the Sydney psyche; each one has a distinct character. Some attract families, picnickers, frisbee throwers, and volleyball players. Others draw dedicated surfers; one or two are frequented by furtive (or not so furtive) nudists. Some beaches are crowded and boisterous; others are secluded and little known, found only after hiking along wooded trails.

Sydney's shoreline is convoluted and would extend for some 350 km (218 miles) if drawn out in a straight line. Beaches are divided into two main types: ocean beaches, which face out to sea and have stronger surf; and harbor beaches, which line Sydney Harbour and tend to be more tranquil.

Luck plays a big part in Sydney life. The city was more or less founded by a stroke of luck, when British Captain Arthur Phillip moved the so-called First Fleet (the first ships of colonization) to the virtually unknown Port Jackson. Phillip had been told to colonize Botany Bay, further south, but he didn't like the look of it. The new settlement around Port Jackson almost perished, but luck held out, and with it the fondness for gambling that has typified Sydneysiders ever since.

Today, Sydneysiders bet an average of over A$850 a year each, on everything from lotteries to slot machines and horseracing. If you're really lucky, you might "win a motza on the lotto"—"motza" being slang for a large amount of money. Australia's best-known manmade structure, the Sydney Opera House, was actually financed by a lottery, and the state of New South Wales derives over 10% of its tax revenue from gambling. Sydney's newly opened casino, Star City, offers 200 gaming tables and 1,500 poker machines. Known as "pokies," slot machines have invaded virtually every neighborhood pub.

At work or play, Sydneysiders are a friendly bunch. "G'day, mate!" is a cheery greeting, sometimes followed by "how ya goin', alright?" Many Australian slang terms are unique, as likely to baffle a Briton or European as an American. "Yakka," for instance, means work. The happy-go-lucky expression "she'll be right" has been largely supplanted by "no worries," but they both mean the same thing—"don't worry, it will all turn out OK!"

Sydney's cultural mix is still evolving, with Britain and the US being the main influences. British visitors notice the rather

As Australian as Yogi Bear

On Sydney's outskirts, a huge theme park called Australia's Wonderland offers Hanna Barbera Land, where "all your favorite Hanna Barbera cartoon characters including Yogi Bear and Fred Flintstone come to life." Australians are as familiar with these characters as are Americans. US sitcoms and cartoons, ranging from "The X-Files" to "South Park," are incredibly popular, and most Sydneysiders of appropriate age are so familiar with shows like "The Beverly Hillbillies" and "The Addams Family" they can hum the theme tunes.

Sydney's Central Station: due to be linked by rail to the airport by May of 2000, in time for the Olympic Games.

Californian style; American visitors are struck by the surprising Britishness of aspects of city life. Both elements are present. Students at Sydney private schools wear blazers and boater straw hats like their counterparts in England; cricket is played on local greens; and if you stroll past Sydney's Supreme Court in downtown Macquarie Street, you can see lawyers in flowing black gowns and horsehair wigs, who would be at home in London's central criminal court, the Old Bailey.

Yet not far away, in George Street, young Sydneysiders visiting cinema and entertainment complexes look straight out of Los Angeles. Shirts and hats bearing US sports emblems are as common in parts of Sydney as in New York. Baseball is growing in popularity.

Many ethnic influences are at work. As US President Bill Clinton observed during a 1997 visit, Sydneysiders trace their origins "to more than 140 different nations—not far short of the 197 different national groups represented in the

Olympics." This diversity is recent. The opening up of Australia since the end of World War II to immigration from all sources, under the slogan "populate or perish," has transformed Sydney to the point where one-quarter of the city's population now comes from a non-English speaking background. After English, the city's main languages are Chinese, Arabic, Italian, and Spanish.

From a society of meat-and-potato eaters and beer drinkers, Sydney has been transformed into a multicultural society with a Mediterranean flavor. Locals are often found sipping cappuccinos or white wine these days rather than knocking back schooners of the amber fluid. ("Amber fluid" means beer, mate, and a "schooner" is a 15-ounce glass.) Basic tastes do, however, persist in Sydney's working-class west. There, the Blacktown Workers Club sells more draft beer than any other bar or beer-hall in the world. Patrons drink over 1 million liters (264,172 US gallons) per year.

Sydneysiders and tourists alike frequent Circular Quay. A magnificent view of the Opera House is just one of its draws.

A BRIEF HISTORY

What Sydney's history lacks in length, it makes up for in color. In two centuries of existence, the city has had more than its share of wild characters. They include tyrants like Captain Bligh, notorious commander of the warship HMS Bounty, who survived a shipboard mutiny to find himself dispatched to Sydney as Governor of New South Wales.

A lesser-known figure was James Hardy Vaux, charming pickpocket and swindler, transported in chains from England to Australia three times—a record. Each time Vaux managed to return to England, they sent him back again, first in 1801 for stealing a lady's handkerchief, next for robbing a jeweler's shop, and the third time for forging bank notes.

Bennelong, the first Aborigine to learn English and wear clothes, was a more respectable individual. (He was also the first Aborigine to drink rum, but that's another matter.) Bennelong traveled to London, where King George III (in one of his saner moods) gave the Aborigine a coat. The tribesman returned to Sydney in 1795 and lived in a hut on the point where the Opera House now stands.

Dreamtime Echoes

Australia has been populated by modern humans for longer than Western Europe—possibly twice as long. Australia's original inhabitants are thought to have arrived between 40,000 and 60,000 years ago during the great Pleistocene Ice Age, crossing a land bridge from Southeast Asia. When Cook landed, the area around Sydney was inhabited by the Eora people, one of 600 or so Aboriginal tribes dwelling in Australia. These tribes spoke many languages, some utterly dissimilar to each other. The word Eora, in the local Sydney language, simply meant "humankind."

An 1870s gold miner's house attests to the harshness of life during that period of Australian history.

For millennia, Aborigines lived within tribal boundaries they believed had been created by hero ancestors in a period called the Dreamtime. Dreamtime legends detail the significance of every tree, rock, and river and explain how humans can live in harmony with nature. Aboriginal trading paths and trails ran throughout Australia's huge landmass (about the same size as the continental US, excluding Alaska) and were often invested with ceremonial or magical qualities. They connected important waterholes, food sources, and landmarks.

Aborigines built no permanent structures but lived in a manner that ensured their survival in the harsh and arid environment of the Outback. They foraged, fished, and hunted kangaroo, wallaby, goanna lizards, and other native beasts with spears and boomerangs. They ate berries, roots, and insects like the witchetty grub (a large white grub about the size of a finger) and the bogong moth; the latter two were roasted on open fires before consumption. (Traditional Aboriginal food has gained popularity recently as "bush tucker," served in specialist restaurants; see page 96.)

Colonists in Chains

In 1770 renowned English navigator Captain Cook spied the hills of eastern Australia and, reminded of the landscapes of southern Wales, coined the name New South Wales. He landed on Australia's east coast and explored Botany Bay, a short distance south of where Sydney now stands and today the site of Sydney Airport's third runway. Cook claimed all the territory he charted for King George III. While the Dutch (and possibly the Spanish, Portuguese, and Chinese) had visited Australia before him, Cook's arrival was to have the greatest effect.

The British soon decided that Australia was an ideal place to send convicts. In the late 18th century, Britain's prisons were bursting, and when the American War of Independence inconveniently interrupted the orderly transportation of convicts to America and the Caribbean (where they were used as virtual slave labor on plantations), the government decided Sydney would be the perfect penal colony. Britain at one stage had declared that 223 offenses were punishable by death (including the crime of "breaking down the head or mound of any fish-pond"); in practice, however, people were

Irish Influence

The transportation of convicts from Britain helped make Australia the most Irish country outside Ireland. After British troops crushed the Irish rebellion of 1798, thousands of suspected rebels were tortured, hanged, or transported. In 1800, almost all white Australians were English by birth or ancestry. Just eight years later, more than 20 percent were Irish.

hanged for only 25 of these, leaving plenty of convicts to be transported to one of the farthest-flung corners of its Empire.

The first shiploads of "prisoner-colonists" arrived in 1787. Under the command of retired naval officer Captain Arthur Phillip, the First Fleet consisted of eleven vessels carrying 1,030 people, including 548 male and 188 female convicts. The convicts were repeat offenders; their crimes generally involved theft. None were murderers—for that, you were hanged.

Phillip anchored in Port Jackson (named but not visited by Cook), which he described as "the finest harbor in the world." The fleet sailed into Sydney Cove, a semi-circular bay that is now known as Circular Quay and flanked by the Opera House.

To the Eora on shore, the sight of a fleet of ships under full sail was so utterly alien that the vessels might have been spaceships from the stars. As Captain Cook had no-

ticed seven years before, Aborigines showed no fear when they sighted a large sailing ship. When long-boats were lowered, full of sailors rowing, the Eora re-acted. A big ship was in-comprehensible; a small boat with men in it was something they could un-derstand. The arrival of light-skinned foreigners created wonder and conster-nation. Rumors spread that

Remembrance of things past: these ghostly settlers recall the early colonists.

one of the pillars supporting the sky had fallen, spilling stars and strange spirits to earth.

In the first few months of its existence, the fledgling colony of petty thieves, sailors, and soldiers ran headlong into famine. Starvation threatened, but Britain continued to send new shiploads of colonists.

Back in Britain the Home Secretary, Lord Bathurst (a Sydney street is named after him), declared he wanted criminals to regard the threat of transportation to Australia as "an object of real terror." It was made clear to all that colonial Governor Phillip was authorized to summarily jail, flog, or hang anyone in New South Wales. Britain sent a Second Fleet to Sydney in 1790—then a third. Merciless floggings with naval cat-o'-nine-tails whips (generally administered about 40 lashes a time, but sometimes over 100) kept a semblance of order—even if the punishment sometimes killed the recipients.

Rum Legacy

Relations with the Eora and other Aboriginal tribes soured as rum and diseases introduced from the west took their toll. Between 1788 and 1890, Australia's Aboriginal population declined from at least 300,000 to about 50,000. (Sydney's Aboriginal population dwindled to just a few hundred by the end of the last century, as many Aborigines fled their traditional lands. Today, less than one percent of the city's population is Aboriginal.)

When Governor Phillip retired, the military took over. The colony's top army officer, Major Francis Grose, cornered the rum market. His troops, nicknamed the Rum Corps, made fortunes in liquor racketeering. Sydney became one of the hardest-drinking settlements in the world, addicted to fiery Brazilian aguardiente and cheap spirits distilled in Bengal. Tradesmen were frequently paid in rum.

London eventually sent out a harsh disciplinarian to shake up the rum-sodden militia. Captain William Bligh was famous well before his arrival, having been set adrift in a longboat after the notorious mutiny on the warship HMS *Bounty* in 1789. Rather than perish at sea as the mutineers had expected, Bligh and his 18 companions had sailed from Tahiti to Timor, a journey of about 6,400 km (4,000 miles), one of the longest voyages ever accomplished in an open boat. When Bligh was appointed Governor of New South Wales in 1805, his legendary temper soon earned him the nickname Caligula, after one of the most hated and feared Roman emperors.

On 26 January 1808, as Bligh was toasting the 20th anniversary of Sydney's founding, a group of his officers mutinied and took him prisoner. The Rum Rebellion, as the uprising became known, deposed Bligh and held him under arrest for a year. London sent a talented Scottish officer, Lachlan Macquarie, to arrest the rebels. Bligh's career was unblem-

The HMS Bounty, once captained by notorious tyrant William Bligh, until the equally infamous mutiny in 1789.

ished by all this—he finished up a vice-admiral—but he lost the governorship of New South Wales to Macquarie.

Macquarie's Vision

Life in the new colony improved under Macquarie's progressive administration and Sydney began to look more like a real town than a military encampment. Thatched huts along muddy roads gave way to properly built schools, churches, a hospital, and a courthouse. Francis Greenway, a convicted forger whom Macquarie had pardoned, became the colony's official architect. He turned out to be highly talented. Many of Macquarie's reforms were resisted by London, which couldn't reconcile his civilizing efforts with the original concept of creating a hellish environment that filled criminals with dread.

The transportation of prisoners continued halfway into the 19th century, but was eventually outpaced by free immigration. In 1849, when one of the last convict ships docked in Sydney Cove, its presence provoked outrage among Sydney's "respectable" citizens. The ship arrived at the same time as several other vessels carrying free immigrants. Even so, the descendants of convicts outnumbered free settlers in Sydney until well into the 20th century.

The Gold Rush

In the 19th century, fortune smiled on Australia. In 1813, explorers crossed the Blue Mountains to the west of Sydney and found a land of endless plains—dry country, but arable. In 1851, beyond the Blue Mountains and 200 km (130 miles) from Sydney, a veteran of the California gold rush struck gold at a settlement named Ophir. (The gold medals for the Sydney 2000 Olympics have been minted from gold mined in this region.)

The gold rush helped shape the history of modern Australia, reversing the exodus of Australians to the California goldfields and bringing an influx of new settlers to the Australian colonies. In 1851, the population of New South Wales was just 187,000. Nine years later it had nearly doubled to 348,000.

Shortly after the Ophir bonanza, prospectors from Melbourne struck gold at Ballarat, triggering an invasion of adventurers from Europe and America, which lifted Australia's population to 1 million by 1860. Life in the goldfields was rough and uncompromising. Miners endured flies, heat, water shortages, and extortionate taxes. Hundreds of prospectors arrived in Australia from China, where New South Wales was known as "New Gold Mountain." Their arrival unleashed local racist sentiment, which endured well into the 20th century. Racially based immigration controls—the infamous White Australia Policy—remained in force from 1901 to 1972.

A Nation Emerges

Australia's island continent remained a collection of separate colonies until 1 January 1901, when in the final year of her reign Queen Victoria permitted the colonies to unite and form a new nation, styled The Commonwealth of Australia. The new country bowed to the Queen as head of

The Bushrangers

Highway robbers, horse thieves, and assorted outlaws fanned out across Australia in the 1850s, and the gold rush served to raise the stakes. Among the most notorious was Ned Kelly. A one-time cattle rustler, Kelly's gang pulled off spectacular robberies, mostly in Victoria. His most memorable incursion into New South Wales was in 1879, when the gang kidnapped the population of the town of Jerilderie while trying to make a getaway after a bank robbery. A year later, an unrepentant Ned Kelly went to the gallows. Thousands mourned, for Australia loves a rebel. "Such is life," were Ned's last words.

Land ho! History revisited in the USA gallery at the National Maritime Museum.

state, and its final legal authority rested with the British Sovereign's private council in London. Although the latter arrangement has changed, Britain's reigning monarch is still Australia's head of state and is depicted on all coinage. Britain's Union Jack flag dominates Australia's flag. There have been moves to remove these colonial vestiges, but so far without success.

Australia has yet to become a republic, although it is moving that way. Australians considered themselves British until well into the 20th century. In World War I, Australian and New Zealand troops formed the Australian and New Zealand Army Corps (ANZAC) to fight Germany alongside other British Empire soldiers. On 25 April 1915, the Anzacs landed at Gallipoli (now located in Turkey) in an ill-conceived diversionary operation that cost the lives of 8,700 young Australians, with

19,000 wounded. More than 60,000 Australian soldiers were killed in World War I, with 152,000 wounded. No other country suffered as high a loss in proportion to its population. The carnage had a major effect on Australia's psyche. Anzac Day, April 25, is a national day of remembrance.

The Iron Lung

Between the world wars, Sydney devoted its energies to building the Harbour Bridge, which gained the nickname "Iron Lung" because it employed hundreds of workers and kept families breathing (in financial terms) during the Depression.

During World War II, Japanese warplanes repeatedly bombed Darwin in Australia's north, enemy submarines penetrated Sydney Harbour and sank a ferry (the torpedo had been fired at an American warship), ships were sunk off the New South Wales coast, and a couple of shells hit Sydney's eastern suburbs. Almost one in three Australians taken prisoner by the Japanese died in captivity. American forces under General Douglas Macarthur arrived in Australia in 1942, and a US force supported by Australia defeated the Japanese decisively in the Battle of the Coral Sea in May of that year.

Cultural Melting Pot

At least a quarter of Sydney's population is born outside Australia. A 1998 study showed 1.4 million people, or a quarter of the population of New South Wales, were born in one of 200 overseas countries. The report revealed that 17% of the state's population spoke a language other than English, with Cantonese the fastest-growing non-English language.

The biggest source of immigration into NSW remains the United Kingdom, which contributes about 20% of the migrant intake, followed by New Zealand (6.3%) and Italy (4.8%). Most new immigrants end up in Sydney.

After the war, Britain aligned itself with Europe and down-graded its ties with the old Empire. As Britain's regional power declined, Australia looked increasingly to the US. Australian troops (over 40,000 of them) fought alongside the US in Vietnam, sparking vehement anti-war protests in Sydney and other Australian cities. Australian Prime Minister Harold Holt introduced the draft and promised US President Lyndon B. Johnson that Australia would go "all the way with LBJ" Holt later disappeared while swimming and may have been eaten by a shark.

Cosmopolitan Country

Sydney has finally taken off as a cosmopolitan international city. The process took about 30 years and coincided with Sydney's evolution as Australia's main financial center, a position formerly occupied by Melbourne. This hasn't been without cost. For one thing, Sydney has lost some of its reputation for egalitarianism. Disparities between rich and poor have grown—and the city's rich love to flaunt their wealth.

Immigration from Italy, Greece, the former Yugoslavia, and elsewhere expanded the city's horizons and cuisine. Culture also took off—innovative dance, drama, and music are flowering. Sydney is set to become Australia's first Eurasian city. Between 1986 and 1991, the number of British-born Sydney residents declined by 5% while the number of Chinese, Koreans, Filipinos, Japanese, and Sri Lankans more than doubled. Immigration flows fluctuate, but demographers say one Sydneysider in five will be all or part Asian within a decade. Many Vietnamese arrived after the Vietnam War, followed by immigrants from Thailand, Cambodia, the Philippines, and Hong Kong. Cantonese is expected to take over as Sydney's second language, displacing Arabic. But if you speak only English, "you'll have no worries, mate!"

Historical Landmarks

circa 60,000 B.C.	Aborigines migrate to Australia from southern Asia
1606 A.D.	Dutch navigator Willem Jansz lands in Cape York.
1688	English pirate William Dampier visits Australia's west coast.
1770	James Cook claims New South Wales for Britain.
1788	First Fleet of British convicts and soldiers arrives.
1808	Governor William Bligh deposed in Rum Rebellion.
1809	Governor Lachlan Macquarie appointed.
1849	Transportation of convicts to New South Wales ends.
1851	Gold discovered near Bathurst.
1876	Last Tasmanian Aborigine dies after decades of conflict with settlers.
1901	Britain allows its Australian colonies to unify into one nation. White Australia Policy introduced.
1915	ANZAC soldiers storm ashore at Gallipoli in disastrous military misadventure.
1932	Sydney Harbour Bridge opens.
1942	Japanese bomb Darwin heavily, then lose Battle of Coral Sea.
1946	Australia conceives "Populate or Perish" immigration program.
1956	Olympic Games held in Melbourne.
1962	Aborigines given right to vote.
1965	Australia enters Vietnam War.
1973	Sydney Opera House opens.
1975	Governor General (Queen's representative in Australia) sacks Australia's elected Prime Minister.
1983	Australia wins America's Cup Yachting Race.
1986	Australia constitutionally severed from the United Kingdom.
1995	Sydney opens its first legal casino.
2000	Sydney Olympic and Paralympic Games.
2001	Centenary of Federation.

WHERE TO GO

Many of Sydney's essential sights are grouped conveniently close together. The harbor is the city's essence
—spanned by the great bridge and adorned by the shell-like
sails of Sydney Opera House. A harbor view dramatically lifts
the price of Sydney real estate, even if you have to crane your
neck to see the water. Sydneysiders flock to the harbor to celebrate great events. They turned out here to greet Queen Elizabeth II (the British monarch, not the ship) on her first visit to
Australia in 1954, and they were here again in January 1988 to
celebrate the bicentenary of the First Fleet's arrival, which
marked the founding of modern Australia.

New Year Celebrations, sometimes tumultuous, take place in
the historic Rocks area near Sydney Harbour Bridge each year.
The arrival of the new millennium and Sydney's Olympic Year,
2000, is likely to produce the most joyous celebrations of all.
Each Boxing Day (the day after Christmas Day), thousands of
Sydneysiders line the harbor to watch the start of the grueling
Sydney to Hobart yacht race, which in 1999 claimed six lives.

To see the harbor at its best, it's worth taking a helicopter
ride or catching the elevator to the top of Sydney's tallest
structure, Sydney Tower. From here, you can see the harbor's
fingers reaching towards the city's west. Sydney Tower is
currently festooned with large, wirework athletic figurines
and an advertising sign. After the Olympics, with a bit of
luck, they will go.

SYDNEY HARBOUR

The best way to see the harbor is to get out on it. Fortunately,
that has always been easy—Sydney runs numerous public
ferryboats from Circular Quay (called Sydney Cove in the
days of convict settlement) providing a fast and cheap means

From Sydney Cove to Circular Quay: a stunning view of the city's skyline, framed by the blue of sea and sky.

of seeing the city's most attractive aspects. In addition to being vital links for commuters, the ferries and high-speed JetCat catamarans are bargains for tourists. About 150 companies operate cruises around the harbor on some 300 boats and ships. Many of the operators invested their money in anticipation of a boom in tourist traffic from Asia, leaving some sumptuous bargains afloat.

Landside, **Circular Quay** is frequented by buskers, artists, and a few "living statues" who appear to be cast in bronze or aluminum—until they move. Circular Quay railway station provides quick connections to Kings Cross and to points in the central city, as well as to the outlying suburbs. The Quay (as it's often called) is a major bus terminal and an easy place to hail a cab.

As you approach Circular Quay from the sea, you are confronted by the Cahill Expressway, a monolithic highway cutting straight across the view. Proposals surface periodically to reroute this highway underground, but no government has dared confront taxpayers with the enormous cost.

The Rocks

The Rocks, just west of Circular Quay, is touristy and souvenir-dominated in some parts, quaint and fascinating in others. The birthplace of Sydney—the First Fleet ended its journey from England here in 1788—this district was a squalid slum in the 19th century, harboring an evil gang of cutthroats known as the Rocks Push. Many of the precinct's original houses were torn down in 1900, when the area was hit by an outbreak of bubonic plague. It killed nearly 100 people. Plenty of historic buildings survived, only to be threatened in the 1960s by developers wanting to level the whole place and replace it with high-rise buildings. A "Save the Rocks" campaign, backed by the union movement, only just prevailed.

It's worth visiting the **Rocks Visitors Centre**, at 106 George Street, before setting out to explore. Graphic displays and free pamphlets provide insights into the area's his-

---

Traversing the Bridge

Before the Sydney Harbour Bridge was built, the city's North Shore could be reached only by ferry, and ferry services were stretched to capacity. The cost of building the bridge has long since been met, but a road toll remains in place. If you cross the bridge in a cab, the $2 toll is added to your fare. For a pleasant short excursion, catch a train from Circular Quay to Milsons Point on the north shore. This five-minute trip of just one stop involves a scenic journey across the bridge. Alight at Milsons Point and walk back across the bridge, using the footway on the bridge's eastern side. The views are sensational.

---

tory. **Cadman's Cottage** (110 George Street) is Sydney's oldest house, a simple stone cottage built in 1816 and occupied for many years by the Governor's boat crew. John Cadman, a pardoned convict, was the original coxswain. A former police station at 127 George Street is decorated with what is perhaps one of the most telling reminders of the convict era—a stone lion's head wearing an imperial crown and clenching a police-issue truncheon in its jaws.

A few steps down from the Visitors Centre, the **Museum of Contemporary Art** gives new life to an Art Deco building formerly used by the Maritime Services Board. Few other art museums enjoy such a view! Displays change regularly and the café on the terrace facing Circular Quay and the harbor is excellent.

Walking north from Cadman's Cottage up Argyle Street you arrive at the so-called **Argyle Cut**, a road carved through sandstone cliffs by convict labor-gangs working with pickaxes. They started in 1843 and finished 18 years later. At the top of Argyle Cut, Cumberland Street provides access to Sydney Harbour Bridge via Cumberland Steps.

"We Got the Convicts..."

Throughout most of white Australia's history, convict ancestry was regarded as a matter of shame, to be concealed if possible. The country's prison legacy was considered a stain on the national character. In the past 30 years, however, a reversal has occurred. Sydneysiders have grown proud of their city's rough-and-tough, no-nonsense past. An aspect of this new-found pride was expressed vividly in a letter to the editor of the *Sydney Morning Herald* in 1998. Commenting on the behavior of US Congress during the impeachment proceedings against Bill Clinton, the correspondent wrote to thank God "that we got the convicts and the Americans got the Puritans."

A Museum with a View: the Museum of Contemporary Art gives new life to an old Art Deco building.

A little further on, in Argyle Place, you will find a neat row of terraced houses straight out of Georgian England. Three grand old pubs in this area deserve mention. The quaint **Hero of Waterloo** at 81 Lower Fort Street was built on top of a maze of subterranean cellars to which drunken patrons were lured, to be sold as crew members to unscrupulous sea captains. That practice has died out but the cellars remain. **The Lord Nelson**, a square sandstone block of a building at the corner of Kent and Argyle streets, was built about 1840 and has maintained a British naval atmosphere ever since. It brews its own beers, some of them pretty strong. Old Admiral ale has an alcoholic strength of 6.7% (over 13 proof). **Palisade Hotel** at 35 Bettington Street was built later than the other two establishments, but retains a pleasant colonial atmosphere, enhanced by expansive harbor views and a fine restaurant.

For history without the refreshments, visit the **Garrison Church**, officially named the Holy Trinity Anglican Church, which dates from the early 1840s. As the unofficial name indicates, it was the church for members of the garrison regiment, the men in charge of the convict colony. It's now a fashionable place to get married.

Back down at the start of George Street, close to the Irish-influenced Mercantile Hotel, **The Rocks Market** takes place each Saturday and Sunday under a 150-m- (492-ft-) long canopy. Musical groups and street entertainers perform, while stall-holders sell crafts, leatherwear, souvenirs, toys, and gifts. Farther up toward the bridge, the Customs Officers Stairs lead down to some charming harborside restaurants housed in old bond stores, fronting Campbells Cove.

☛ Sydney Harbour Bridge

With its drive-through stone pylons (purely ornamental) and colossal steel arch, Sydney Harbour Bridge triumphantly spans

Sydney Harbour Bridge was a major engineering feat of its time, and remains a well-loved city monument today.

the harbor. The bridge stars on television each New Year's Eve, when it serves as a platform for a spectacular fireworks display. Some 1,600 rockets are fired from the arch in a computer-controlled sequence, while other fireworks positioned on the roadspan create a Niagara-like cascade into Sydney Harbour. New Year's Eve arrives in Sydney before it does in most other major world cities, and therefore Sydney's display usually leads international television coverage of New Year's Eve festivities.

Before the Sydney Opera House opened in 1973, the bridge was the most internationally recognized symbol of Sydney. Completed in 1932, the bridge was to have been opened by the Premier of New South Wales, but just as that worthy gentleman approached the official ribbon brandishing his pair of golden scissors, an unauthorized Irish horseman rode through the crowd and slashed the ribbon in two with a saber. The mounted protestor declared the bridge open in the name of "the decent citizens of New South Wales." It was a bizarre initiation for a Sydney icon that was intended to be the world's longest single-span bridge—it was beaten just four months before its opening by New York's Bayonne Bridge, which is just 63 cm (2 ft) longer.

Sydney Harbour Bridge, which took nine years to build, was one of the foremost engineering feats of its day. Some 1,400 workers toiled on the 503-m (1,651-ft) structure. Sixteen lost their lives. Repainting the bridge is a 10-year job, using 30,000 liters (almost 8,000 US gallons) of paint. Once finished, it's time to start again. Paul "Crocodile Dundee" Hogan worked on this monotonous task for years before discovering there was more money—and more satisfaction—in show business.

Nicknamed the "Coathanger," the bridge is equipped with a cycleway (on the western side), as well as a walkway, road lanes, and a railway line. For a small fee, you can climb the 200 stairs inside the south-east pylon for panoramic views.

There's a little museum there, too. The stairs are reached via Cumberland Street in the Rocks.

The bridge's role is less crucial now that you can drive under the harbor through a tunnel. The tunnel trip is faster but boring. Guided climbing tours of the bridge now allow you to walk right over the huge over-arching span (see page 87).

☛ Sydney Opera House

Standing on the western side of Circular Quay and gazing east, the viewer is confronted by one of Sydney's most delightful buildings, now adjacent to one of its most loathed.

The first, of course, is the Opera House, with its wondrous billowing sails. The second, infinitely less inspiring, is a new A\$200-million apartment block contemptuously nicknamed "the Toaster" by Sydneysiders and denounced by architectural experts around the world. The Toaster encroaches on the Opera House's space and deprives it of some of its dramatic splendor.

Moves to level the Toaster are growing. The NSW Premier, Sydney's Mayor, and Australia's Prime Minister have all denied any responsibility for the intrusion, which at least shows they don't approve of it. Veteran campaigner Jack Mundey, who

---

A Drop for Connoisseurs

Above the Argyle Cut, on Cumberland Street, the Australian Hotel is well worth a visit. A friendly pub in the older Aussie tradition, it stocks beers from every state in the country, including a few eagerly sought by connoisseurs. The Australian is one of only two pubs in Sydney to serve unfiltered beers created by master brewer Geoff Scharer. These include Picton Lager (5 percent alcohol) and the celebrated Bavarian-style Burragorang Bock (6.4 percent), acclaimed by expert tasters and seasoned journalists as possibly the best beer in Australia.

The famous Opera House, Sydney's pride, was financed almost entirely by lottery proceeds.

helped save much of the Rocks district from demolition in the 1970s, now chairs the Save East Circular Quay Committee, which is fighting to have the Toaster flattened.

Not even the Toaster can spoil the **Sydney Opera House**, though. Covered in a million gleaming white tiles, this extraordinary building does the seemingly impossible and embellishes a perfect harbor. While it's hard to imagine the harbor without it, Sydney Opera House nearly wasn't built at all. The design was one of 233 entries submitted in a contest to find an ideal building for the site, which had previously been occupied by a squat, turreted depot for tramcars.

As the contest progressed, several banal entries (including one resembling two giant shoeboxes) were short-listed. Danish architect Jørn Utzon's vision for the site, the eventual winner, was at first discarded. Fortunately, however, Utzon's plan was spotted by accident in a pile of rejects by US architect Eero Saarinen, one of the judges. Saarinen recognized the plan's potential and brought it to the attention of his less perceptive colleagues.

Utzon moved to Sydney to oversee construction, but endless bickering with petty officials and enormous cost overruns took their toll and he resigned from the project in 1966, returning disillusioned to Denmark. The interior plan was subsequently handed over to a committee of Australian architects. Utzon has never returned to see the finished work. In a conciliatory gesture, he was officially invited back in 1998 to oversee some reconstruction, but he declined.

The Opera House was originally budgeted at A\$7 million, but ended up costing 13 times that. In true Sydney style, the shortfall was raised by a lottery. Despite its cost, the finished project was immediately hailed for its grace, taste, and class. Elegance extends from the tip of its highest shell-like roof, which soars 67 m (221 feet) to the Drama Theatre's orchestra pit, situated several meters below sea level.

Strictly speaking, the term Opera House is a misnomer. The building's opera theater (seating 1,547) is fairly small and not entirely satisfactory, although its intimacy helps some productions. Its concert hall (seating 2,697) is the biggest of five halls. The Opera House offers two restaurants: Bennelong and the Harbour Restaurant. It's worth taking a guided tour of the whole building. Tours depart about every 30 minutes from 9:15am to 4pm each day, except for Christmas Day and Good Friday.

☛ Royal Botanic Gardens

Next to the Opera House, Sydney's lush **Royal Botanic Gardens** (established in 1816) offer an extensive collection of Pa-

Stop and smell the roses or simply sprawl on the lawns at the Royal Botanic Gardens, where you are invited to do either.

cific plant life, parklike lawns, a pretty little restaurant tucked away in the greenery, and some wonderful picnic spots. A sign in the gardens is worth quoting: "Please walk on the grass. We also invite you to smell the roses, hug the trees, talk to the birds, sit on the benches, and picnic on the lawns. This is your Garden, and unlike most botanic gardens overseas, admission to the Royal Botanic Gardens is free." (A slot for donations is provided in case you are inspired to generosity.)

Sublime views of Sydney Harbor can be enjoyed in Royal Botanic Gardens from **Mrs. Macquarie's Chair**, a sandstone rock ledge carved in 1816 for the wife of Sydney's best-loved Governor. Mrs. Macquarie's Chair stands beside Mrs. Macquarie's Road on Mrs. Macquarie's Point. (You couldn't go far wrong in early 19th-century Sydney by naming geographical features after the Governor's wife!) The view from Mrs. Macquarie's Chair, looking west across Farm Cove to the Opera House, is one of the world's most photographed. Here, nature and architecture meld beautifully, with the Royal Botanic Gardens forming a perfect backdrop to the splendor of the Opera House. The gardens would greatly enhance the Opera House view from West Circular Quay, too—were they not also obscured by the unsightly Toaster development.

Beside the gardens, and separated from them by the Cahill Expressway, is **The Domain**, another of Sydney's wonderful open spaces. Given over to amateur orators on Sundays (rather like Speakers' Corner in London's Hyde Park), The Domain is also home to the **Art Gallery of New South Wales**. The original building, dating from 1897, has a formal exterior decorated with much bronze statuary; light-infused modern extensions added in 1988 provide sweeping views of east Sydney, part of the harbor, and the suburb of Woolloomooloo. (A spelling teaser for Sydney schoolchildren, Woolloomooloo was threatened by wholesale demolition in the 1970s, but was saved by resident protests and union "green bans.") An afternoon at the Art Gallery will give you a crash course in more

Bats in Procession

The large flocks of bats you often see flitting through Sydney skies are called gray-headed flying-foxes. Weighing up to a kilogram (2.2 pounds) each and known to scientists as *Pteropus poliocephalus,* the bats fly over the city at dusk to dine on figs and other soft fruit. Watching a flock on the wing, silhouetted against an awesome orange and mauve sunset, is one of Sydney's priceless experiences. The bats, with their furry, foxy faces, frequent the Royal Botanic Gardens and Centennial Park, but their main camp is at Gordon, a leafy suburb on Sydney's North Shore.

than a century of traditional and modern Australian art. The Yiribana Gallery there is devoted to Aboriginal art and Torres Strait Islander art. The Asian and South Pacific sections are also impressive. The museum provides guided tours and, when you need a break, an inviting café-restaurant awaits.

DOWNTOWN SYDNEY

Sydney's city center, universally called the **CBD** (for Central Business District), includes a magnificently restored 19th-century emporium, several delightful Georgian sandstone edifices, some fine Victorian structures, and a vast number of high-rise buildings. A few recent skyscrapers are notable and some are even elegant, but most belong to the so-called "international egg-crate" school of architecture—bland modern buildings that were erected mainly in the 1960s and 1970s.

At 305 m (1,000 ft), **Sydney Tower** at Centrepoint is the city's highest vantage point. From this 1970s pinnacle you can relish a superb 360-degree view of Sydney and its surroundings. On a clear day you can spot Terrigal Beach, 100 km (62 miles) north, and the Blue Mountains far to the west. On a scale of world towers, Sydney Tower is slightly taller than Munich Tower and a little shorter the Eiffel Tower. Sydney's version is unusual in that it has no communications function. It houses a revolving restaurant and an observation deck.

The city's main square, **Martin Place**, is flanked by the imposing Victorian Renaissance-style General Post Office (GPO) building. No longer a working post office, this structure was recently converted into a 418-room, five-star Westin hotel. During World War II, the GPO's clock tower was dismantled for fear that Japanese bombers might zero in on the landmark; it was restored 20 years later.

From the same era as the GPO, but even grander, the **Queen Victoria Building** (QVB) occupies an entire block on

Queen Victoria in her own building: this century-old master-piece is now a splendid shopping center.

George Street (Sydney's main street and the oldest street in Australia) opposite Sydney Town Hall. The Byzantine-style QVB began as a municipal market and commercial center, including a hotel and a concert hall, topped by statuary and 21 domes. Built in 1898 to commemorate Queen Victoria's Golden Jubilee, this splendid building was later downgraded into offices and a library. In the 1960s, small-minded officials decided to demolish the QVB to make way for a car-parking building. Fortunately, the authorities ran short of money, the demolition was put on hold and the building was spared. It was faithfully restored in the 1980s to create a magnificent all-weather shopping center housing nearly 200 chic boutiques, cafés, and restaurants, in a cool and unhurried atmosphere of period charm. Pierre Cardin has called it "the most beautiful shopping center in the world."

For an instructive comparison, contrast the QVB with the Hilton Hotel building in George Street immediately opposite. The Hilton structure, an unlovely concrete monolith, dates from the 1970s, when the QVB was still under threat of demolition. The Hilton building's saving grace is its basement **Marble Bar**, a Beaux-Arts masterpiece of a pub, much older than the Hilton itself. A cornucopia of Victorian paintings, stained glass, marble and mirrors, the Marble Bar was preserved when the Hilton was built.

Macquarie's Sydney

The CBD's only real boulevard is **Macquarie Street**, laid out by Governor Macquarie and running from East Circular Quay near the Opera House to Hyde Park. This relatively short street, filled with historic buildings, is well worth the walk.

Starting at the northern end, Macquarie Street flanks **Government House**, open from Friday to Sunday. This extraor-

---

Paddy's Market

Chinatown, at the southern end of Sydney's CBD, is the home of Paddy's Market, over 150 years old but recently housed in a new purpose-built venue. Paddy's is a mecca for weekend bargain hunters. More than 1,000 stalls sell everything from fish, mangoes, Chinese herbs, and sacks of onions to T-shirts, hot dogs, watches, shoes, jewelry, and souvenirs. It's open 9am to 4:30pm Fri, Sat, and Sun. Chinatown is full of inexpensive eating houses. At large Asian emporiums there, numerous food outlets share the same seating, crockery, chopsticks, and cutlery. Thai, Cambodian, Chinese, Japanese, and Malaysian cuisine are all served in adjoining food booths. A tasty bargain.

dinary mock-Gothic castle, complete with crenellated battlements, was designed in 1834 by Edward Blore, architect to King William IV. Continuing south along Macquarie Street brings you past the Ritz-Carlton Hotel on the righthand side (formerly Sydney's venereal disease clinic), and BMA House, a splendid Art-Deco edifice.

Farther down on the left, the **State Library of New South Wales**, bordering the Domain, consists of two harmonious buildings, one old, one new, linked by a walkway. Classical columns announce the main portal of the old Mitchell Wing, built in Greek-revival style in the early 20th century, while the adjoining 1988 concrete-and-glass addition boosts the building's size and spirits. The next building is **State Parliament House**, an elegantly colonnaded building that has resounded with political debates (and much invective, not all of it sober), since 1827. It's open for visits and admission is free.

Sydney Hospital superseded the Rum Hospital of the early colonial days, so named because Governor Macquarie granted three locals permission to import 45,000 gallons of rum (for sale at a huge profit) provided they built him a hospital. Outside the hospital, a bronze statue of **Il Porcellino**, a wild boar, replicates a 17th-century original in Florence. The statue was donated by an Italian immigrant whose relatives had worked at the hospital. Patting its snout is said to bring good luck. Just inside the hospital grounds, a curious green-and-yellow fountain embellished with brightly colored flamingos and swans is intended, presumably, to lift the spirits of recovering patients.

The Mint next door, originally the Rum Hospital's south wing, was converted into a mint to process gold-rush bullion midway through the 19th century. In the early days it was used to produce "holey dollars"—Spanish coins recycled to ease a desperate shortage of cash. The new colony used the equivalent of both the doughnut and the hole: the centers were punched

New meets old; skyscrapers frame a historic building in the Sydney Central Business District.

out and used as 15-pence coins, while the remaining outer rings became five-shilling coins, worth four times as much.

Immediately opposite, a gargantuan brown block-like building houses the **State and Commonwealth Law Courts**. This modern contribution to Macquarie Street, utterly out of scale with the opposite side of the street, is adorned with Australia's coat of arms—an emu and kangaroo each trying to look fierce. The forecourt is enlivened at times by the arrival of barristers in gowns and wigs.

Hyde Park Barracks, next to the Mint, was commissioned by Governor Macquarie to house 600 convicts. It was designed by Francis Greenway, pardoned forger and architectural genius. Completed in 1819 and adorned with a fine colonial clock, this is perhaps the best Georgian building in Sydney. At various times it housed "unprotected females" and Irish orphans. A convict dormitory with hammocks has been reconstructed on the third floor and you can stay there overnight, although there is a long waiting list. Convicts were less enthusiastic about their stay there.

A computer base on the third floor of Hyde Park Barracks gives public access to the records of every prisoner who passed through the institution. More detailed records, covering virtually everyone ever transported to Australia, are available at the State Library of NSW, a few blocks further down Macquarie Street.

Hyde Park, at the end of Macquarie Street, is a fraction the size of its London namesake, but it provides the same green relief. The land was cleared at the beginning of the 19th century, with a race track being its first big attraction.

Interior of the stately St. Mary's cathedral, which stands on the site of the colony's first Catholic church.

Hyde Park was the venue for boxing matches, and was also the new colony's first cricket pitch. The two most formal features of these 16-hectare (40-acre) gardens are the **Anzac War Memorial**, commemorating Australia's war dead, and the **Archibald Fountain**, an extravaganza of statuary on mythical themes, with a fine plume of water.

Sightseers who enjoy old churches should mark three targets on the edge of Hyde Park. To the north, the early colonial **St. James's Church** on Queen's Square was designed by Francis Greenway as a courthouse. When its use was changed, the intended cells were converted into a crypt. Across College Street to the east, **St. Mary's Cathedral** stands on the site of the colony's first Catholic church, and from the same era, the magnificent **Great Synagogue** faces the park from the opposite side, across Elizabeth Street.

The **Australian Museum**, on College Street facing Hyde Park, was established in 1827, very early after settlement, largely so scientists could show off Australia's unique flora and fauna. Distinguished architecturally by massive Corinthian pillars, the museum is still strong on natural history. You can learn a lot about Australian birds and insects, and view a few local dinosaurs. The section dealing with human evolution is well worth browsing—and don't miss the giant cockroaches on the second floor.

DARLING HARBOUR

Darling Harbour, a vast tourist and leisure center built by decree in time for the 1988 Bicentennial celebrations, offers parks, a light and airy shopping complex, a Convention and Exhibition Centre, restaurants, and museums.

The whole Darling Harbour area was formerly derelict docklands. Its rehabilitation was the biggest urban renewal program in Australian history. Despite its closeness to Sydney's center, Darling Harbour has never been fully integrated with the central city. It lies alongside the CBD like an island. Linking the CBD with Darling Harbour's diverse elements is the **Monorail**, whose elevated track covers a 3.5 km (2 mile) loop of eight stations. Dubbed the "Monsterail" during construction, this conveyance has always been controversial; critics consider its track and pillars a blot on the cityscape. Views from the Monorail are vastly preferable to views of it, and the carriages have become even more kitsch since the operators decided to cover them in garish advertising. While the Monorail is seriously flawed as a public transport system, it's an amusing sightseeing vehicle, resembling the one at Disneyland. A recorded commentary with an advertising theme tells you where you are.

To reach Darling Harbour from the city, you are probably better off walking across Pyrmont Bridge, which runs off the end of Market Street. The bridge is built of wood and was the

Monster cockroaches

The world's largest cockroaches live on the second floor of the Australian Museum, on the east side of Hyde Park. The giant burrowing cockroach or rhinoceros cockroach (*Macropanesthia rhinoceros*) is native to Australia. It dwells in woodland and feeds on dead dry eucalyptus leaves, growing up to 10 cm (4 inches) long and weighing up to almost 50 grams (1.75 ounces), or about the weight of an AA-size battery. Species in the Central and South American jungles may be a little longer, but none are as massive. The live specimens in the Australian Museum dwell in a large, comfortable glass tank in a section of the museum devoted to children (and devoid of insect spray). These giant roaches are harmless, wingless, and very robust. Schools in North Queensland (where the roaches come from) keep them as pets.

*Darling Harbour and the Monorail; once derelict docklands,
this area is now a vast tourist and leisure complex.*

first electrically operated swing-span bridge in the world. It
was more elegant before the Monorail ran across it.

On the western side of Darling Harbour, Harbourside
Shopping Centre offers more than 200 shops and food outlets. Shops sell gemstones, fashions, souvenirs, gifts, Aboriginal art, and much else. Dining options range from cheap
and cheerful snacks to stylish seafood dining at Jordons.

Diagonally opposite on the eastern side of Darling Har-
bour is **Cockle Bay Wharf**, a more upmarket development
which opened in November 1998. Cockle Bay features five-
star eateries, little cafés and coffee shops, and a new pub,
Pontoon. Restaurants include Ampersand (Sydney foody
Tony Bilson's latest establishment, see page 140), Nick's
Seafood and Coast (both are speciality seafood restaurants),
Tiara (the first of Japan's best-known chain to open outside
Japan), and Chinta Ria Temple of Love (established by Mel-

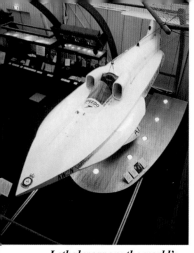

Lethal weapon: the world's fastest boat on display at the National Maritime Museum.

bourne-based Malaysian restauranteur Simon Goh).

Next door to Harbourside Shopping Centre, the **Australian National Maritime Museum** attracts more than 120,000 international visitors a year. Housed in a towering white building with a wave-form roof, the museum displays more than 2,000 maritime-related objects in permanent and temporary exhibitions. A fleet of 12 historic vessels lies moored at wharves outside.

The **Panasonic Imax Theatre** in Darling Harbour has what may the world's largest screen—it's 10 times larger than those found in traditional cinemas. The ground floor features a retail store with an Australian-inspired selection of gifts and merchandise, and the **Wockpool** restaurant, a 250-seat restaurant and noodle bar from which diners can gaze out at Darling Harbour and the Sydney skyline. Nearby **Sega World Sydney**, an indoor family theme park, offers nine major rides, some 200 audio-visual arcade games, live entertainment, and a bustling food court.

Darling Harbour's Exhibition Centre is designed on the suspension bridge principle, with cables attached to masts holding up the roofs. Outside it, **Tumbalong Park** offers open spaces, brilliantly original fountains, geometrical challenges, swings, slides, and mazes; it's way ahead of conventional children's playgrounds.

At the western end of Darling Harbour is the circular concrete **Sydney Entertainment Centre**. Designed for sports events, concerts, and other public festivities, it can hold 12,500 spectators. Next door is the **Pumphouse**, a historic building that once supplied hydraulic pressure to operate lifts and the weighty doors of bank vaults. Recently restored, it now serves as a tavern for thirsty tourists.

Darling Harbour's **Chinese Garden**, officially called the Garden of Friendship, was a joint effort by the governments of New South Wales and the Chinese province of Guangdong. This one-hectare (2.5-acre) garden allows quiet walks and contemplation amid apricot, azalea, jasmine, and weeping willow trees overhanging paths, ponds, and rock formations.

Aboriginal Art and Culture

The **National Aboriginal Cultural Centre** (NACC) opened in 1998 in its new Darling Harbour venue, not far from Sega World Sydney and the Chinese Garden. The center attracts oversees visitors and Australians alike by providing an authentic look at Aboriginal art and life.

The NACC's overview of Aboriginal and Torres Strait Islander culture and crafts is drawn from more than 200 Aboriginal communities Australia-wide. The center includes a 180-seat dance theater; a fine-arts gallery with exhibitions changing monthly; a historic photo gallery; and an arts and crafts center. The NACC is operated as a joint venture between a private company and various representative Aboriginal communities. A trust of Aboriginal people manages their community's shareholdings in the center, and verifies the cultural integrity and authenticity of all presentations.

The center presents a collection of experiences that reflect the history and culture of the Aboriginal people. Theater/dance performances lasting 30 minutes are held each day at 11am, 1pm, 4pm, and 6pm. Each performance is narrated by a "storyteller" in the tradition of Aboriginal oral history. Entry to the center, art gallery, arts and crafts and photo gallery is free but there is a charge for theater/dance performances. Open daily 9:30am to 8pm.

Super-Aquarium

Sydney Aquarium, on the city side of Darling Harbour, is one of the largest aquariums in the world. Perhaps start with the crocodiles, whose baleful immobility seems to challenge crowds to hang around until one of them stirs. Or head first to the Open Ocean Oceanarium, where you can go face-to-face with sharks that weigh up to 300 kg (660 pounds) and measure over 9 m (30 ft) long. The aquarium has 146 m (480 ft) of underwater tunnels. The newest attraction is the Great Barrier Reef Complex, which includes an oceanarium, live coral caves, a coral atoll, and a tropical touch-pool; altogether, the complex houses over 6,000 animals from the Great Barrier Reef off of Australia's northeastern coast.

KINGS CROSS

Bright lights and shady characters exist side by side in Kings Cross, a couple of railway stops from circular Quay. "The Cross," as it's often called, is Sydney's version of Paris's Pigalle or London's Soho—neon-filled, a bit tacky, crawling with hedonists and counter-culturalists of all persuasions. Action continues 24 hours a day, with a diverting cavalcade of humanity: the bizarre, the flamboyant, the drugged, and the drunk—if it's excessive, it's here. On weekends tourists flock to the Cross to glimpse a bit of weirdness. Sometimes, the weirdest characters they spot are other tourists.

The Cross is a favorite venue for "Buck's Nights," boisterous bachelor parties held the night before a man gets married.

Don't miss Sydney Aquarium, one of the largest in the world, and surely one of the most well-appointed.

The Cross's main drag is **Darlinghurst Road**; bohemian verging on sleazy, it's dotted with a jumble of bars, strip joints, fast-food outlets, tattoo parlors, and X-rated book and video shops. The **Bourbon and Beefsteak Bar** near El Alamein Fountain is a fun place for a few drinks. It was highly popular with American servicemen on R&R leave during the Vietnam War. Doormen at the Bourbon and Beefsteak keep the area's seedier residents at bay (most of them, anyway). Early in 1999, the establishment gained brief publicity when the cricketer Ricky Ponting, a well-known name in Australia, was knocked out during a late-night dispute on the premises.

Kings Cross is famous (or infamous) for its "spruikers" (pronounced sprookers)—fast-talking salesmen who hang around the doors of strip clubs and try to lure passers-by inside. Predictably, their main targets are single men or men in groups.

They tend to leave mixed-sex couples or mixed-sex groups alone—you hope. Retailers in the area consider spruikers a deterrent to business and periodically campaign to have them suppressed. Fortunately, the attention span of most spruikers is very brief; they'll only demand your attention for a few seconds.

You're also likely to encounter prostitutes plying their trade from doorways in the Cross. "Like a girl, love?" is their customary greeting. Prostitution is legal in Sydney, provided streetwalkers observe rules such as staying away from schools, churches, and private homes. Brothels exist in Kings Cross, Surry Hills, and elsewhere throughout the city. The Cross has a thriving drug trade, which has survived all attempts to eradicate it, but you probably won't be offered drugs unless you seek them.

A five-minute walk from Kings Cross Station, **Elizabeth Bay House** is a magnificent home built in 1835 for the colonial

Kings Cross: unassuming, perhaps, by day, but buzzing all night with strip joints, clubs, and all manner of hedonism.

secretary in the style of a Grecian villa. It serves as a reminder that Kings Cross was fashionable for at least a century. In the years after World War II, wealthier residents departed and less reputable elements moved in. Many former grand homes in the Cross have been converted to backpacker lodgings.

Victoria Street, which runs parallel to Darlinghurst Road, is a quieter alternative to the main strip. It's lined with gracious old homes, trendy cafés, and fine restaurants. In the 1970s, Victoria Street became a battleground, with residents and unions pitted against rapacious property developers—the latter seeking to demolish homes to build high-rises. Juanita Nielsen, a celebrated Sydney heiress who edited a newspaper called *Now,* was a valiant campaigner for preservation. Although her efforts helped avert much high-rise ugliness, Ms. Nielsen roused the ire of unscrupulous developers. She disappeared in July 1975 and was never seen again.

ELEGANT PADDINGTON

An inner-city suburb worth investigating is Paddington, to the southeast of Kings Cross. Intricate wrought-ironwork, commonly known as Sydney Lace, is the local trademark; it adorns the balconies of many 19th-century terraced houses. Paddington was developed for workers' housing in the 1880s, but fell into dilapidation and by the 1940s had become a slum. A slow process of gentrification then began, and by the 1970s "Paddo," as the locals call it, had become a fashionable, rather artsy place to live.

The suburb is now fully gentrified, with residents more likely to be lawyers or stockbrokers than artists. Houses usually fetch over A$1 million and local real estate is still appreciating rapidly. The adjoining suburb of Woollahra, studded with mansions and consulates, is even more leafy and patrician. You would be hard-pressed to pick up a house in Woollahra for a mere million.

Paddington offers plenty of ethnic restaurants, antique shops, art galleries, fashionable bookshops, and trendy boutiques. One of Sydney's best public markets, Paddington Bazaar, is held each Saturday on the grounds of Paddington Public School on Oxford Street. It offers every type of art and craft and is enlivened by street entertainers (you can cash travelers' checks in the main hall).

Oxford Street is a center for Sydney's burgeoning gay community, with the Albury being the street's longest-established gay pub. **Juniper Hall** on Oxford Street is Australia's oldest surviving example of a Georgian villa. Completed in 1824, it was built by the convict settler Robert Cooper, described as a "distiller, publican, and self-confessed smuggler," who lived there with his third wife, Sarah, and their many children. Formerly concealed by a row of mediocre shops built in the 1930s, Juniper Hall fell into disrepair until it was bought in 1984 by the National Trust of Australia and restored. The undistinguished row of shops was demolished while Juniper Hall survived, an inspiration to the locals. Next to Juniper Hall, Underwood Street leads to Heeley Street, a pleasant downhill walk that emerges 10 minutes later into Five Ways, with its pubs, shops, and galleries.

Oxford Street is home to two of Sydney's best bookshops, Ariel and Berkelouw, and three of its more imaginative cinemas, the Chauvel, the Verona, and the Academy Twin.

Victoria Barracks, which was built by convicts to house a regiment of British soldiers and their families, is Oxford Street's renowned example of mid-19th-century military architecture.

Centennial Park

In 1811, the far-sighted Governor Macquarie set aside an area outside the city for public use, naming it Sydney Common. The Governor's original 405-hectare (1000-acre) bequest has been much whittled away since, alas, but Centennial Park at the eastern end of Oxford Street south of Woollahra is a welcome remnant. Centennial Park has provided greenery and fresh air to city folk since 1888, when it was dedicated on the centenary of Australia's foundation to "the enjoyment of the people of New South Wales forever."

The park's 220 hectares (544 acres) of trees, lawns, duck ponds, rose gardens, and bridle-paths are visited by about three million people a year, who cycle, roller-blade, walk their dogs, feed birds, throw frisbees, fly kites, picnic, and barbecue.

If you'd rather hoof it than stroll, hit the bridle paths of Centennial Park.

Centennial Park, and Lachlan Swamp within it, support large numbers of birds. Among the many distinctive species are long-beaked ibises, which look like something off the wall of an ancient Egyptian tomb but are in fact native to Australia. Flocks of loud-squawking, sulfur-crested cockatoos regularly make their presence known. Bats twitter in the park's venerable Moreton Bay fig trees, and possums (the native Australian type) dwell in the date palms. The palms themselves are under threat from a mysterious virus and are being progressively replaced with more resistant species.

If you fancy a ride on the bridle path, check with Moore Park Stables, Tel. (02) 9360-8747. Bicycles and pedal-carts can be rented from Centennial Park Cycles, Tel. (02) 9398-5027.

Centennial Park Kiosk, a lovely setting for a meal and a glass of wine, was renovated and expanded in 1998. Beside it stands a charming, if curious, modern stone fountain, incorporating an illuminated crystal that changes color at night. Another park ornament, Federation Pavilion, is a ponderous, round, pillared structure with a bronze roof. Built in 1988 as part of the Bicentennial celebrations, it is inscribed with the cryptic motto: "Mammon or Millennial Eden," a poet's question about which direction Australia is headed.

Not far from the Pavilion, Centennial Park Amphitheatre provides an outdoor venue for events and productions. In the summer months, a popular Moonlight Cinema program is held in the amphitheater. Films start at about 8:45pm and tickets are available at the gate from 7:30pm or in advance from Ticketmaster (Tel. 136-100); for screening details, tel 1900-933-899.

Restored elegance in gentrified Paddington, where property costs a pretty penny.

Adjoining Centennial Park, Moore Park houses the Sydney Cricket Ground (a landmark to cricket fans around the world), Sydney Football Stadium, and the Equestrian Centre.

In a contentious move, two hectares (five acres) of Moore Park were recently requisitioned for the Eastern Distributor Tollway through inner Sydney, a project scheduled for completion in 2000. More controversy followed when another 24 hectares (59 acres) of the park were handed over to US media tycoon Rupert Murdoch's Fox Group, for redevelopment into a studio and entertainment complex. Fox Studios is being built on the former Royal Agricultural Society Showground, where the Royal Easter Show was held for decades, before being moved to a new site next to Sydney Olympic Park at Homebush.

INNER SUBURBS

Bohemian Newtown

Newtown, in Sydney's Inner West, 4 km (2.5 miles) from the CBD, is today's version of what Paddington was in the 1960s. Newtown's cosmopolitan nature and its high proportion of students (many attending the University of Sydney, just down the road) give the suburb an artistic temperament. Originally, Newtown consisted of farms on the outskirts of Sydney. Its inhabitants in 1838 were listed as "877 Protestants, 364 Roman Catholics, one Pagan and one Jew." German and Italian shopkeepers set up businesses there in the early 20th century. By the 1970s, Newtown had become a cheap-rent suburb housing a large proportion of new immigrants.

Today, students, hippies, gays, lesbians, black-clad goths, New-Age traders, and young families share the precinct, which has developed into a lively and entertaining quarter of delis, cafés, bookshops, second-hand clothing and retro-fashion outlets, pubs, and multicultural restaurants, many of them offering excellent value. Some of the Thai restaurants have flippant names like Thai Foon (though the ultimate joke name, Thai Tanic, isn't in Newtown but over the other side of the harbor at McMahons Point).

Retail outlets on King Street, the suburb's main road, tend to be small scale, typified by All Buttons Great and Small, which sells just that—buttons. The locale around the northern end of King Street has moved upmarket but the gentrification has been contained, so far.

Gould's Book Arcade at 32 King Street is a huge emporium chock full of second-hand books. The shelving system is a bit haphazard there, but you can come up with surprising bargains if you are prepared to "fossick" (an Australian term for search). The Sandringham Hotel (known as the Sando) was once infamous as one of the loudest music venues in Sydney, specializing in ear-splitting rhythm-and-blues bands. Its loud-music license was recently revoked; talented bands and musicians still perform here, but in a quieter mode. The Southern end of King Street takes on a Pacific Island flavor at weekends, when Sydney's Polynesian and Melanesian population heads there to shop for Pacific Island spices and produce.

Newtown has some great pubs and bars. Kuletos at 157 King Street serves dynamite cocktails, including a formidable version of Long Island iced tea, which combines vodka, tequila, gin, white rum, triple sec, lemon juice, and a dash of Coke, all in a single glass. Drinks are half-price between 6pm and 7:30pm each evening and between 9pm and 10pm on Thursdays. The Newtown Hotel and the Imperial Hotel are both gay pubs; the Imperial is the pub from which the bus departed in the movie *Priscilla: Queen of the Desert*. Lesbians favor the Bank Hotel on King Street.

Balmain

Balmain, which is close to the CBD and easily accessible by ferry (from Wharf 5 at Circular Quay to Darling Street Wharf), is located on a peninsula and retains a sense of separateness from the city. From Balmain, the CBD looks so close you would think you could drive straight there across the harbor. You can't, though, and a road sign points this out to newcomers. The drive to the city is considerably more circuitous.

Well into the latter half of the 20th century, Balmain was staunchly working-class. The suburb was settled by sailors and boat-builders in the 1840s, and pubs have always been popular. In the 1880s there were 41 taverns in Balmain; now there are 24. Balmain has become the abode of successful actors, lawyers, and others who can afford the steep property prices. Its village character survives, however, and its working class traditions have not entirely died out, as a visit to the Balmain Leagues Club will attest.

Balmain's main street is Darling Street, where the trendy London Tavern stands more-or-less opposite St. Andrews Congregational Church. A lively flea market takes place around the church on Saturdays, with all sorts of ethnic food stalls (Egyptian, Indian, Lebanese, vegetarian, and others) arranged in the church hall and rows of stalls outside selling arts, crafts, and second-hand goods. Often a band will entertain—a Romanian Gypsy trio, for instance.

The walk from Darling Street to Sydney Harbour is memorable, passing pubs, neat little terrace houses, sandstone cottages dating from the early 19th century, quaint shops, and renovated warehouses. Louisa Road (technically in the neighboring suburb of Birchgrove) is one of Sydney's top real-estate strips, with no shortage of millionaire's town houses.

Leichhardt

Not far from Newtown, the suburb of Leichhardt has been a base for Sydney's Italian community since the 19th century. First it hosted just a few Italian groceries. By 1962, four Italian cafés had sprung up, and other Italian stores followed. Fewer than five percent of Leichhardt's current population was born in Italy, but many residents of Italian extraction live in the suburb, which retains a strong Italian flavor. Norton Street is the best place to browse; eateries include Bar Baba, Bar Italia, Caffe Sport, and La Cremeria. Norton Street Markets, a warehouse full of Italian produce, sells everything from sun-dried tomatoes and prosciutto to wines, olive oils, and balsamic vinegar.

Parramatta

Further west, Parramatta is almost as old as Sydney. In the 1790s, many of Sydney's administrative functions and all its farming efforts were moved up-river to Parramatta, where the soil was more fertile. Governor Phillip declared he would have founded the colony in this spot if he had known about it earlier. In 1804, a group of 260 Irish convicts led a rebellion at Parramatta aimed at overthrowing the Governor, but troops crushed the uprising. Most of the conspirators were hanged.

Many Parramatta buildings are new and not particularly inspiring, but a few places of interest remain, including Elizabeth Farm, Old Government House in Parramatta Park, and Experiment Farm cottage. For the most pleasant, and most scenic ride to Parramatta, catch one of the RiverCat catamaran ferries at Circular Quay.

HARBOR EXCURSIONS

 The ferry ride from Circular Quay to **Taronga Zoo** (formerly called Taronga Park Zoo) is pleasant and takes only about 12

Who doesn't love them? Koalas can be spotted at Taronga Zoo, which is situated in natural bushland.

minutes. Most tourists view their first kangaroos and koalas at the zoo, situated in natural bushland at Bradleys Head, Mosman. The setting can't be beat: if you choose your vantage point carefully, you can photograph the heads of giraffes against a background of CBD cityscape, including the Opera House.

Designers at the zoo have worked to ensure that the animals live in sympathetic surroundings reminiscent of their natural habitats. The Nocturnal House features indigenous night-time creatures illuminated in artificial moonlight, unaware of onlookers. The Rainforest Aviary houses hundreds of tropical birds. If you arrange your visit around feeding times, which are posted at the gate, you can watch the keepers distribute food while they deliver talks about their charges. The zoo has an active educational program; there's even a performing seal.

Fort Denison occupies a small harbor island known as "Pinchgut," which originally served as a prison. Troublesome convicts endured a bread-and-water diet and sometimes even worse. In 1796, a murderer was hanged on the island and his body gibbeted for three years as a warning. Fort Denison contains a martello tower (a circular masonry blockhouse), a barracks, and gun battery, all dating from the 1850s. The buildings have been restored so weddings and cocktail parties can take place in this macabre, if scenic, venue.

THE BEACHES

Sydney has some 70 beaches, offering everything from raging surf to small, caressing waves. Use plenty of sun-screen (ultraviolet readings are high) and heed the advice to swim only between the red-and-yellow life-guard flags, which indicate patrolled sections of beach. Strong currents and tidal

Weird Waddlers

The Echidna and Platypus House at Taronga Zoo allows you to view these reclusive Australian monotremes (egg-laying mammals) close-up. The waddling, spine-covered echidnas dine on ants and termites. The duck-billed platypus is even more peculiar, having astonished observers since explorers first laid eyes on it. When 18th-century zoologists in London received their first stuffed and preserved specimens, they doubted anything that weird could exist. Most experts considered it a composite fake, assembled by Chinese taxidermists for sale to gullible seafarers. The platypus is the size of a small cat, with a broad bill and webbed feet like a duck. It is amphibious, covered in fine fur, possesses milk-secreting glands, lays eggs, and dines exclusively on mud, from which it extracts tiny plants and animals. Not until 1884 was the platypus declared a mammal.

rips run periodically along many Sydney beaches; drownings are an unfortunate feature of summer. Drowning between the flags, however, is virtually unheard of—there have been only two cases in Australia since the world's first surf lifesaving club was formed at Bondi Beach in 1906.

Bondi Beach

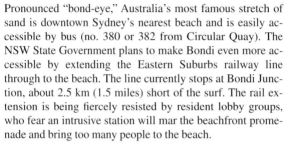

Pronounced "bond-eye," Australia's most famous stretch of sand is downtown Sydney's nearest beach and is easily accessible by bus (no. 380 or 382 from Circular Quay). The NSW State Government plans to make Bondi even more accessible by extending the Eastern Suburbs railway line through to the beach. The line currently stops at Bondi Junction, about 2.5 km (1.5 miles) short of the surf. The rail extension is being fiercely resisted by resident lobby groups, who fear an intrusive station will mar the beachfront promenade and bring too many people to the beach.

Site of surf shops, cafés, and lively al fresco restaurants, Bondi has been popular ever since trams started running there in 1894. Its appeal has outlasted the trams. Style purists consider Bondi's appearance a bit tacky, but its fortunes are climbing and the suburb has become quite fashionable. James Packer, son of Australia's wealthiest man, publisher Kerry Packer, maintains quarters at Bondi, as do other Australian celebrities. Bondi Pavilion, which houses dressing rooms for 5000 people, a grand ballroom, and other vital beach facilities, displays photos of the beach dating back to the mid 19th century, when it was privately owned and utterly deserted.

Backpackers use Bondi to celebrate Christmas riotously and see in the New Year. Mainstream beach-users include lithe and leathery veteran sun worshippers, fanatical surfers, and families at play. The cliffs around Bondi's southern end

Worship the sun, hit the surf, and check out the scene: Bondi Beach has room for all—and dressing rooms for 5000!

offer a bracing walk and enchanting views, especially in the early evening by the light of a full moon.

South from Bondi, **Bronte Beach**, backed by palms and Norfolk pines, has plenty of facilities and en extensive park for picnicking. **Coogee Beach** is better than most for swimming.

Vaucluse Peninsula and South Head

The peninsula jutting north from Bondi to Watsons Bay and culminating in South Head offers superlative beaches and great walks. Sydney's most expensive residential real estate is located around here, in Vaucluse (just south of Watsons Bay), and in Point Piper (a peninsula to the west of Vaucluse, separated from it by the almost equally wealthy suburb of Rose Bay).

The Bondi and Bay Explorer bus (see Public Transportation in A to Z) allows you to travel on a scenic tour from Circular Quay to Watson's Bay, where you can get out and admire Pacific Ocean views from the Gap, a dramatic seafront cliff. Houses in the Vaucluse/Watsons Bay area are lavish but tasteful, with occasional exceptions to each of those criteria. The winding streets are bougainvillea-lined, and the surroundings have a secluded, villagey sort of charm. All along the route you'll catch splendid views of the city. Camp Cove is where Captain Phillip first stepped ashore in Sydney Harbour (on 20 January 1788) after abandoning Botany Bay further south. The captain had taste—the beach at **Camp Cove** is one of Sydney's finest. A plaque notes where Captain Phillip landed.

Vaucluse House, a stately home with its own beach in the pretty suburb of Vaucluse, adds its mock-Gothic turrets to Sydney's harbor skyline. The mansion began as the home of a colorful convict, Sir Henry Brown Hayes, the Sheriff of Cork before he was banished to Australia for the abduction of his bride. In the 1830s the new owner, William Wentworth, expanded it into a 15-room homestead.

Not far south of Watsons Bay is **Nielsen Park**, full of shady trees and one of Sydney's top spots for picnicking and swimming. Nielsen Park has its own excellent little bay—which is generally referred to as Nielsen Park Bay rather than its real name, Shark Bay. The beach is shark-netted (netting was introduced in the 1930s), so you needn't fear any risk of being nipped. If you feel like nipping into some food, a kiosk serves snacks and good espresso. The headland towards Vaucluse Point (to the right of the beach when you face the sea) is often quite secluded, even on public holidays.

Northern Beaches

Cheerful **Manly** is reached from Circular Quay by ferryboat or high-speed Jetcat catamaran across Sydney Harbour. The jet-cats are quicker, but the ferry is more relaxing. Manly offers a choice of two beaches—one open to the ocean and popular with surfers, the other a calm harborside crescent suitable for children. The area was named by Governor Phillip, who thought the Aborigines sunning themselves on the beach had a commanding ("manly") presence.

Linking the two beaches, the lively Corso is a Mediter-ranean-style promenade, lined with tourist souvenir stores, fish and chip shops, fast-food emporia, and ice-cream stands. Manly maintains a holiday atmosphere and has for decades used the slogan, "Seven miles from Sydney—and a thousand miles from care." The motto has resisted metrication.

The oceanside beach, divided into North Steyne and South Steyne, is lined with Norfolk Pines and pleasant cafés. If you walk south along South Steyne, you end up at Shelly Beach Park, with a sheltered little beach perfect for children. The park is an enchanting and romantic place at sunset, when the sky turns red and gold and the view includes ships far out to sea.

At **Oceanworld Manly** (to the left of the ferry terminal as you arrive), divers hand-feed sharks and giant stingrays every day—an awesome spectacle. Oceanworld Manly denizens include jumping Australian and New Zealand fur seals (star performers) and a giant cuttlefish with three hearts and green blood. A moving walkway traverses an acrylic tunnel surrounded by freely swimming sharks, rays, and their friends.

North of Manly, a couple of Pacific beaches with charming names, **Curl Curl** and **Dee Why**, offer good surfing. **Collaroy** and **Narrabeen** are linked by a single beach with an ocean pool, ideal for families. **Newport Beach** is a beautiful, broad sweep of sand. **Avalon Beach** is known for surfing and popular with children. At the northern tip of the Sydney beach region, **Palm Beach**—the abode of millionaires, successful actors, and advertising types—is in a class of its own. Manicured, nicely gardened villas occupy the hills of the peninsula behind Palm Beach. **Whale Beach** is similarly well-appointed.

Cobblers, Obelisk, and Lady Jane

Sydney has several nude beaches. The most accessible is Lady Bay, also known as Lady Jane Bay, near Watson's Bay, just around the bend from Camp Cove. Reef Beach, facing Manly Cove and a long walk from Manly's harborside, has long been favored for discreet nude sunbathing, although residents periodically make objections. Two other nude venues are Cobblers Beach and Obelisk Beach. The first is east of the North Shore's Balmoral Beach; the second is located near Georges Heights, Mosman. Access to Cobblers is easy by boat but difficult by land.

Dress on Sydney's beaches has come a long way over the past century. In the 1900s, public swimming was permitted only in the early morning and after dark. In 1935, an ordinance was passed forbidding men to wear swimming attire that exposed their chests. Beach inspectors were empowered to remove offenders to a dressing enclosure, where they could be compelled to clothe themselves "respectably." By the 1960s, regulations had mellowed considerably, although beach inspectors still prowled the sands searching for excessively brief costumes (the focus by that time had shifted to women). Nowadays, women sunbathe topless on some beaches, including Bondi, but the practice is frowned upon on other, more sedate beaches. "Check whether anyone else is doing it," is a good rule.

OLYMPIC SYDNEY

The Olympic Games last just two weeks but their effects linger. In Sydney's case, the legacy of the 2000 Olympics will benefit the city for centuries through the creation of huge new parks. The main site of the Games, **Sydney Olympic Park** in the western suburb of Homebush, has become one of the city's top attractions for tourists and residents alike. In 1998, **Homebush Bay** attracted 4.7 million visitors—two years before the projected start of the Games on 15 September 2000.

High-speed "Jetcat" catamarans are a common sight in Sydney Harbour.

To make it easier for visitors, a Sydney Olympic Explorer Bus Service makes ten stops in a continuous circuit at all major sporting venues and Bicentennial Park (a big new park near the sporting facilities) at Homebush Bay. Allow a full day if you want to visit each venue at the site. Otherwise, half a day is probably enough. Two guided walking tours of sporting facilities and the Sydney Showground are also available.

A pleasant way of visiting the Olympic venue is to take a combined RiverCat (public catamaran ferry) cruise up the Parramatta River and bus tour of the Olympic site. Sydney Buses sell this as a package at reasonable rates. Tickets are available at Wharf 5 at Circular Quay. They cost 35 percent more on weekends and they sell out quickly because each tour is limited to 39 participants. There are five trips each weekday and two each on Saturdays and Sundays. For further information, dial 131-500.

Millennium Parklands

A magnificent giant has been created from 450 hectares (1,112 acres) of landscaped terrain around the Olympic facilities and the adjoining Sydney Showground. Bigger than New York's Central Park and twice the size of Sydney's existing Centennial Park, Millennium Parklands is one of very few large parks to open within a major world city in the 20th century.

Before the park and the Olympic facilities could be built, a massive clean-up of the Games site was required. This operation, completed in 1998, represented one of the greatest environmental victories in Australia's history. The site had previously served as a saltworks, a brickworks, an abattoir, a naval armaments depot, and a landfill dump. Lost to Sydney through pollution, it has returned to service in a form that would have astounded the salt-workers, brickies, and slaughtermen who used it in bygone decades.

Homebush Bay's checkered history dates from the days when people gave little heed to the ecological consequences of their actions. In the early 1990s, soil studies conducted there revealed 9 million cubic meters (11.8 million cubic yards) of contaminated waste, both on land and deposited in old estuarine channels. More than a quarter of the site's overall 760 hectares (1,878 acres) was polluted with domestic, commercial, and industrial trash. The initial state of the site was so bad, many people could not understand how Olympics Games could ever be held there. But in the end the Games effectively returned to the community a piece of land that had been all but abandoned.

Kakadu, whose wetlands ecosystem faced total decimation, is making a comeback—and so are the birds.

Apart from old waste spills, contractors had to tackle the effects of previous poor usage, which had contributed to soil erosion and weed growth. Wastes were consolidated into four areas and then contained between the underlying clay/shale base and a clean, impermeable 1-m (3-ft) surface cap of clay. Seepage flowing through the containment area was collected in special drains dug into the underlying clay, pumped into tankers and taken to a nearby liquid waste plant for treatment and disposal. By 1994, the work had proved so successful it earned a special award from the Keep Australia Beautiful Council for outstanding achievement in environmental management.

Homebush Bay's wetlands ecosystems had been damaged by removal of native vegetation and extensive landfilling. Native foliage has been replanted and a more natural creek system recreated, with meandering pools to encourage wildlife to return. Studies show birds and fish are coming back, including a regular visitor to Homebush Bay, the Golden Plover, which flies a 22,000-km (13,670-mile) round trip to Australia from Alaska each year to avoid the harsh Alaskan winter. Ten other bird species migrate to Homebush Bay each year from Asia, Siberia, and Alaska.

Olympic Village

When the Governments of Australia and New South Wales bid for the Games in 1993, they committed themselves to ecologically sustainable development (ESD), a concept which aims to protect the environment with a range of initiatives to halt global warming, ozone depletion, and toxic chemical pollution, and to protect biodiversity.

These initiatives included the creation of "the world's most environmentally friendly village," a spacious and pleasant suburb a short walk from the main stadium to house the athletes. The Village is also the world's largest solar-powered suburb, with the capacity to generate more than 1 million kilowatt-hours of power annually. This represents a saving of 7,000 tons

---

VIP Frogs Rule

The rare Green and Golden Bell Frog, a threatened species, makes its home in a disused brick-pit between Bicentennial Park and the Olympic Stadium. This reclusive little amphibian happens to bear Australia's sporting colors. Under the original Olympic site plan, the frog's home was to have given way to the Olympic Tennis Centre. But the 300 or so frogs refused to move, even when a new pond was built for them. As a result, the Tennis Centre was moved and the brick-pit was incorporated into the Millennium Parklands. The brick-pit will be used to store water for the Olympic site's recycled water system—a compromise that won't harm the frogs.

of carbon dioxide each year compared with similarly sized regular homes, plus a 75 percent reduction in electricity use.

Aquatic Paradise

While the colossal, 110,000-seat Sydney Stadium is the dominant landmark at Sydney Olympic Park, it is by no means the
only sporting venue there. The state-of-the-art **Sydney International Aquatic Centre** (SIAC) welcomes everyone for
water sports, recreational swimming, carnivals, and fun. More
than 1.4 million people visited SIAC in 1998. The facility's
leisure pool is especially popular with children; decorated with
palm trees and colorful mosaics, it's equipped with spas, a
river-ride, spray jets, spurting "volcanoes," a water slide, and a
bubble beach. And for serious swimmers, SIAC's other facilities are second to none. The Competition Pool is 50 m (164
feet) by 25 m (82 feet), with 10 lanes and a minimum depth of
2 m (6.5 feet); it's used for long and short-course swimming,
water polo, and synchronized swimming. A movable bulkhead
allows the water area to be divided for various uses such as
canoe polo, scuba diving, and underwater hockey. Underwater
viewing windows provide coaches with an ideal viewpoint for
evaluating training techniques. Photographers like them too.

Sydney Showground

Sydney Showground, next to the main Olympic site, attracted 1.2 million people to the first Royal Easter Show held
there in 1998. The Sydney Storm baseball team holds weekly games there on Friday and Saturday nights. The Showground's ingeniously designed halls and pavilions minimize
the need for air-conditioning and heating.

The State Sports Centre, built on the site of the old Abattoir
saleyards, opened in 1984. It includes the State Hockey Centre,
State Softball Centre, and a golf-driving range, along with

grass playing fields that can be used for staging outdoor events. This multipurpose venue for elite and amateur training and competition can be used for to 26 sports, including basketball, fencing, volleyball, judo, wrestling, and rhythmic gymnastics.

Sydney International Athletic Centre is a two-arena complex built to serve as a warm-up track and training venue for the Games. Its 5,000-seat grandstand is named in honor of Australia's "Golden girl" Betty Cuthbert, four-time Olympic champion. Two 40-m-(131-ft-) high masts towering high above the complex support the 100-tonne roof with high-tensile cables.

DAY TRIPS

Blue Mountains

Rural scenery surrounds Sydney on three sides. The most popular destination—an easy hour's drive or rail trip west of the city—is Blue Mountains National Park, one of the most spectacular and captivating wilderness areas in Australia. The mountains really do look blue, given the right conditions: the blue tint is created by the refraction of light through the haze of volatile eucalyptus oil evaporating from the trees.

You can sign up for one of the many day tours from Sydney, or you can visit and explore at your own pace. Don't expect sharp peaks like those in the Swiss Alps or Wyoming's Grand Tetons—the range is far too ancient and eroded for that. Here, immense, bush-filled canyons and ravines, weathered precipices, deep river valleys, and soaring sandstone cliffs awe the viewer. The main road through the Mountains is the Great Western Highway, which begins its climb through a succession of towns, with the forest yawning below and lines of hills gradually dissolving into the pale blue eucalyptus haze.

Rising to a height of more than 1,300 m (4260 ft), the Blue Mountains offer crisp air, vast sandstone valleys where water-

The awe-inspiring Blue Mountains, so named because of the blue haze created by evaporating eucalyptus oil.

falls shatter on the rocks, gardens that burn with autumn color, English-style homesteads, and little towns of timber and stone. Several grand, old-style hotels (including the sprawling, art-deco Hydro Majestic Hotel, built as a European-style spa in the 1930s) complement historic towns, including Katoomba, Wentworth Falls, Leura, and Mount Victoria.

A day's drive takes in the major attractions. The **City of the Blue Mountains** (comprising 26 towns and villages) is one of the few places in Australia cold enough to snow (occasionally) in mid-winter, usually around August. At that time, one of the Blue Mountains' most photographed rugged sandstone formations, the **Three Sisters**, is sometimes completely covered in snow. Local guesthouses stage "Yulefests" in the winter (July), complete with Santa Claus and traditional Christmas fare; it makes sense climatically, even if it baffles many visitors.

At any time of year, views from **Echo Point** or **Govett's Leap** take the breath away. If you have the time and energy, descend the 841-step **Giant Staircase** at Katoomba and walk the Jamieson Valley to the foot of the **Scenic Railway**, then take the railway back up. The railway is a three-minute hair-raising ride along an old mining cart track with the steepest incline in the world. For an equally exciting excursion across the gorges, try the **Scenic Skyway**, a cable car dangling high above the valley. Katoomba's Maxvision Cinema screens a worthwhile documentary on the region, entitled "The Edge."

Jenolan Caves

Farther along the Great Western Highway, about 60 km (38 miles) from Mount Victoria, is Australia's most famous un-derground attraction. Explorers have yet to penetrate the en-tire labyrinth of Jenolan Caves, but thousands have admired the stalactites and stalagmites of the nine caves open to the public. Guided tours through the spooky but often awesome limestone caverns last about an hour and a half.

THE HUNTER VALLEY

The best-known and most picturesque wine-growing region in New South Wales is the Hunter Valley, a two-hour drive north of Sydney. You can visit it as a day trip, but it's also a very popular destination for weekenders.

Wine making is nothing new to this region. Vines from France and Spain were transplanted here early in the life of the colony, and by the mid 19th century, the region was pro-ducing hundreds of thousands of bottles of wine a year. Re-finements to the production process in this century have resulted in a number of high-quality vintages.

The gateway to the **Pokolbin** region—where most of the Lower Hunter Valley wineries are located—is the town of

Cessnock. Here, the local tourist information center supplies touring maps and brochures. The Hunter's 50 wineries harvest grapes in February and March, but they welcome visitors throughout the year. Pokolbin is one of Australia's most attractive wine-producing regions: neat, rolling vineyards spread from the base of the Brokenback Range.

Most of the Hunter wineries are open for tastings. Major wineries include Tyrell's Wines, Lindemans Winery, Wyndham Estate, the Hunter Estate, Rothbury Estate, and the McWilliams Mount Pleasant Winery. The wines made by big-name producers shouldn't lull you into neglecting limited-edition "boutique" wines, many of which can be obtained only by buying a bottle from the person who tended the vines, picked the grapes, fretted over fermentation, and possibly stuck on the labels as well. The wineries are at their best on a warm summer evening, when the breeze sends a shimmering wave through the green sea of vines.

When not in the vineyards, visitors to Hunter Valley can amuse themselves with horseback riding, cycling, bushwalking, golf, tennis, water sports, and hot-air ballooning. If you're feeling whimsical, try a picnic on a horse-drawn carriage or a bicycle trip along the vine trail.

Hawkesbury River

The Hawkesbury River winds for 480 km (about 300 miles) on its way to the Pacific at Broken Bay, just beyond Palm Beach in the most northerly section of Greater Sydney. The Hawkesbury's gentle waters and ever-changing vistas—coves and bays and steep wooded banks—delight visitors. There's no need to own a boat; there are many places where you can rent one. You don't need a license or any boating experience. Clipper Cruiser Holidays at Akuna Bay in Ku-ring-gai National Park (40 minutes drive from Sydney) rents out 34-ft- (10.4-m-) cruisers, which sleep between two and eight people each. Once you have your vessel, you can spend the day fishing, go ashore to find your own little beach, follow a trail through the National Park, or just lie back on the deck and enjoy a good book.

The Hawkesbury area might have become Australia's national capital. In 1899, an extraordinary, utopian plan arose to build an Australian capital on the Hawkesbury headlands. To be called Pacivica, the city would have included buildings modeled on the Tower of London, Windsor Castle, and other architectural icons of the Empire. (The only thing missing was the Taj Mahal.) As you cruise these gentle secluded waterways, you'll be delighted the plan was set aside.

The Southern Highlands

Lush grazing land and orchards dotted with historic towns and villages lies to the south of Sydney. Towns worth visiting in-

Old Sydney Town, which lies beyond the Hawkesbury River, makes for a charming and relaxing excursion.

clude picturesque **Mittagong** and **Bowral**, a prettily gardened town that holds a popular tulip festival every October. Charming **Berrima** is a Georgian gem so well preserved the whole town is listed as a national monument. Plenty of antique shops, arts-and-crafts galleries, and atmospheric tea shops. Among the most distinguished monuments, the Surveyor General Inn, established in 1834, claims to be Australia's oldest continuously licensed inn. It makes an appealing spot for a drink or a meal. Another landmark, Berrima Gaol, was built in the 1830s by those who were soon to inhabit it.

Canberra

Canberra, Australia's custom-built national capital, lies at the heart of the Australian Capital Territory, a 240-sq-km (93-sq-mile) expanse of farmland, bush-clad mountains,

Sydneysiders tend to frown upon Canberra, Australia's capital, but it isn't all politics—there's plenty of culture here.

forests, and valleys southwest of Sydney. If you plan to visit Canberra from Sydney as a day trip, you are better off flying. Flights are frequent and take just 40 minutes. Buses make the 282-km (175-mile) Canberra/Sydney route daily, but the trip lasts over three hours each way. There are also three trains a day from Sydney.

Many visitors to Australia relegate Canberra to a day trip, only to realize after arrival the city is worth much more. Canberra boasts some of Australia's finest galleries and public buildings, and perhaps the loveliest surroundings of any national capital. Sydneysiders tend to look askance at Canberra, because of the high proportion of politicians and civil servants who live there. But although Canberra's streets are curiously devoid of pedestrians compared to other Australian cities, there is much to commend the capital.

Created in 1901 when Australia decided it needed an independent capital free from political or commercial domination by any one state, Canberra was designed by Chicago landscape architect Walter Burley Griffin, who never visited the site. A planned community created straight from the blueprints, Canberra has no old quarter and few restored historic buildings. The city's most prominent structure, **Parliament House** on Capital Hill, opened in 1988, replacing an earlier building from 1927. Other civic attractions include the Australian National University, the National Film and Sound Archives, the Australian War Memorial, All Saints Church in Ainslie (originally the railway station at Rookwood Cemetery in Sydney before it was moved stone by stone and reconstructed), the Australian Institute of Sport, the Australian National Library, the National Science and Technology Centre, the High Court (open 9:15am to 5pm, for a glimpse of Australian justice), the National Gallery of Australia, and the Old Parliament House.

More than 30 artistic and cultural institutions are located in Canberra, ranging from Questacon (a hands-on facility at the National Science and Technology Centre) to the **National Gallery of Australia** on the banks of Lake Burley Griffin. The Gallery houses the most extensive, and most eclectic, collection in Australia—highlights range from Aboriginal masterpieces to Monet's *Water Lilies* and Jackson Pollock's *Blue Poles.* The capital's other diversions include clubs, music venues, more than 300 restaurants, seven cinema complexes, and a casino.

Language

A highly spiced version of the English language, Australian has its own inventive and amusing vocabulary. Some of the more picturesque phrases, such as "don't come the raw prawn with me" (don't try to fool me) are fading from general usage, but here are a few terms you're likely to hear.

G'day	Hi or Hello ("good day")
Mate	Friend
Tinny	Can of beer
Ocker	Stereotypical, no-nonsense Aussie
Dag	Unfashionable or socially inept person
Ripper!	Expression of approval
Dinkum	Genuine
Cozzie	Swimming suit
Hoon	Loud, aggressive, or stupid person
Root	Sexual intercourse
Dunny	Outdoor toilet
Shout	To buy a round of drinks
Bludger	A lazy person who lives off of others
Garbo	Garbage collector
Pom, Pommy	English person

WHAT TO DO

SHOPPING

Sydney shopping hours generally run from 9am to 5:30pm, Monday to Friday, 9 to 5 on Saturday. Shops do not close for lunch or at any other point during the day. Thursday is late shopping night in the Central Business District (CBD), when many stores stay open until 9pm. Other suburban centers have late-night shopping on other nights. Shops at Darling Harbour stay open until 9pm or 10pm daily.

Acceptance of the big three credit cards (American Express, Visa, and MasterCard) is virtually universal in Sydney, with lesser-known cards accepted only at larger enterprises. International travelers can buy goods duty-free, which involves producing your air ticket and passport at the duty-free store when making your purchase, and not opening the packages before you leave the country. On your departure you have to show them to the customs agent. Tipped off by the computer, he'll be looking for you. (For further information on duty-free allowances, see page 112.)

Where to Shop

In downtown Sydney, skyscrapers sit above subterranean shopping arcades, and **Pitt Street Pedestrian Mall** is linked to several shopping plazas. For shopping in a historic atmosphere, try the **Queen Victoria Building** or the stylish and historic **Strand Arcade**, a Victorian masterpiece running between George and Pitt Streets. Boutiques of some of the world's leading fashion designers are on the upper levels. It's also worth inspecting the jewelry shops at the Strand. For outlet stores and giftware, try **Imperial Arcade** running between Pitt and Castlereagh Streets, the adjacent **Skygarden** and **Centrepoint**, or **Glasshouse** on King Street. Sydney's main department stores are David Jones and Grace Bros. Gowing's is a long-established family emporium, selling good-quality, durable clothing at down-to-earth prices; it caters mainly to men.

What to Buy

Aboriginal art. Aboriginal artists sell their work in art centers, specialist galleries, and craft retailers and through agents. Each traditional artist owns the rights to his or her particular stories, motifs, and totems. Indigenous fabric designs by artists such as Jimmy Pike are eagerly sought. The National Aboriginal Cultural Centre or Gavala, both at Darling Harbour, are good places to start.

Antiques. The Paddington and Woollahra district is full of antique shops.

Worthy pieces to seek out include clocks, jewelry, porcelain, silverware, glassware, books, and maps.

Clothing bargains. The clothing trade is based mainly in the cosmopolitan, inner-city suburb of Surry Hills. Start opposite Central Railway Station and head east for factory outlets. Some shops are open only to the trade, but

The Strand Arcade, yet another place to shop 'til you drop!

South Pacific artworks; quality art and crafts are easy to come by, if you're interested in a genuine souvenir.

others deal with the public. The area around Regent and Redfern Streets, south of the CBD, is another bargain area.

Fashion. Sydney's end-of-season sales hold a bonus for visitors from the Northern Hemisphere. Just as a season is ending in Australia, the same one is about to begin north of the equator. "Wearable art" in swimwear; fashion garments, fabrics, and souvenirs are available from Ken Done shops (named after the artist and designer), Desert Designs, Balarinji Australia, and Weiss Art.

Outback clothing. A distinct style of clothing has evolved in rural Australia, an area collectively known as the "Bush." Driza-bone oilskin raincoats, Akubra hats (wide-brimmed and usually made of felt), and the R. M. Williams range of bushwear (including boots and moleskin trousers) are good examples. Blundstone boots, made in Tasmania and renowned for their durability, are another. Brand names to look for when shopping for bushwear include Country Road, Covers, Trent

Nathan, Lizzie Collins, Studibaker Hawk, Perri Cutten, Von Troska, Jodie Boffa, Scanlan & Theodore, Morissey Edmiston, Collette Dinnigan, Saba, and Robert Burton. Australian merino sheep produce fine fleece ideally suited for spinning. All sorts of knitwear, from vivid children's clothing to Jumbuk brand greasy wool sweaters (which retain the sheeps' natural water resistance), is available throughout the city.

Opals. Australia is the source of about 95% of the world's opals. "White" opals are mined from the fields of Andamooka and Coober Pedy in South Australia, where inhabitants live underground to escape searing summer heat. "Boulder" opals—bright and vibrant—come from Quilpie in Queensland, while the precious "black" opal (actually more blue than black) is mined at Lightning Ridge and White Cliffs in New South Wales.

Sapphires. After opals, sapphires are Australia's most-mined gemstones. A sapphire is exactly the same stone as a ruby—the only difference is the name and the color. Both

Sparkle with a "white," "black," or "Boulder" variety. Australia is the source of about 95% of the world's opals.

are varieties of corundum, a transparent form of aluminum oxide found in metamorphosed shales and limestones. Creative Australian jewelers work wonders with sapphires.

Diamonds. Australia has one of the world's richest deposits of diamonds. The gems are mined by Argyle Diamond Mines in the rugged Kimberley region in the west. Kimberley is famed for its "pink" diamonds, sometimes marketed under the description "champagne." Hues range from lightly flushed to deep red.

MARDI GRAS

Sydney is one of the world's most hospitable cities for gay residents and visitors. The best-known gay and lesbian event in Australia (and the largest gay procession in the world) is the Sydney **Gay and Lesbian Mardi Gras Parade**, which takes place each February and attracts greater crowds than any other event in the country. The climactic finale of a month-long festival of gay art, culture, music, theater, and dance, the parade culminates in a wild party. Tickets to the party are usually sold out before the end of January, but you don't need a ticket to watch the parade.

The prototype of the Mardi Gras parade was a protest march in 1978, held to commemorate the Stonewall riots in New York City. The Sydney march was broken up by police in no uncertain terms, a crackdown that produced the same effect as the infamous police raid on New York's Stonewall Inn. A wave of indignation and fury swept the gay community. A series of protests, with 178 arrests, led the NSW Government to repeal the Summary Offences Act, which had previously made street marches and acts of public affection between males illegal.

Since then, the parade has grown steadily every year; it now features about 100 floats and 5,000 participants and attracts some 600,000 spectators. Regular paraders include

Dykes on Bikes, the Marching Boys, the Marching Girls, the Marching Drags, and the Sisters of Perpetual Indulgence (a group of bearded "nuns"). There is something to please—or shock—everyone.

In 1998, the annual Mardi Gras festival, parade, and party poured A$99 million into Sydney's economy, the largest economic impact of any sporting or cultural event in Australia.

SPORTS

Too much sport is barely enough. That's the way Australians feel about their weekends. If not actually playing or watching sport, Aussies are reading about it, arguing about it, listening to it on the radio, watching it on TV, or betting on it.

Participatory Sports

Golf. A cursory examination of a map of greater Sydney shows that the city is full of parks. Closer inspection reveals that many of these are in fact golf courses. Golf is one of Australia's most popular participant sports, with about 400,000 players out of a population of 18 million. Australian players like Greg Norman, Steve Elkington, and Robert Allenby have boosted the game's popularity. The Australian Golf Club in Sydney was formed in 1882, and thousands of golfers exercise their skills each weekend at 115 courses and driving ranges throughout the city. Nearly half of these are public courses available for a casual game at reasonable rates. Moore Park Golf Course is a pleasant venue within a short cab ride of the CBD, and a number of picturesque courses are scattered throughout the North Shore. Many of the private clubs welcome visiting players, although a member's invitation may be necessary and various conditions may apply, such as green fees, the need to make reservations in advance, or restricted times. Some of the more exclusive clubs have strict dress codes.

Everybody's going surfing…Australia's big breaks make it one of the world's best and most challenging surf spots.

Tennis. Australia has produced many champion tennis players, including Rod Laver, who in 1962 won the Australian, French, Italian, United States, and Wimbledon singles titles, all in the same year. You'll find no shortage of courts or partners in Sydney. Local councils run the courts and the fees are cheap. Check the Yellow Pages on the phone book for a local court.

Skiing. The downhill season in the Snowy Mountains (aka the Australian Alps), south of Sydney near the border with Victoria, usually lasts from June until September, sometimes into November. Contact Tourism New South Wales for details, Tel. 132-077.

Swimming and sunning. With dozens of alluring beaches within easy reach, swimming is a major activity in Sydney. The more popular beaches are marked by yellow-and-red flags showing where it's safe to swim. Beware of strong undertows

Thrillseekers wanted: BridgeClimb takes intrepid walkers over the massive arches of Sydney Harbour Bridge.

or shifting currents and obey the instructions of the lifeguards. If a shark alert is sounded (rare), beat a retreat to the shore. Other dangers are bluebottles, jelly-like hydrozoans that can inflict an agonizing (though non-fatal) sting. Blue-ringed octopuses are more dangerous but rare. Apply sunscreen to exposed skin, wear a hat, and try to stay out of the midday sun.

Scuba diving. North Head is a favorite spot for Sydney scuba divers. There are many other dive sites in New South Wales as well, though none are as spectacular as those of the Great Barrier Reef, that coral wonderland further north. For information on the scuba scene, phone the Australian Underwater Federation, Tel. 9529-6496.

Surfing. Surfing areas are marked by signs, flags or discs. Bondi Beach is the best-known surfing zone in Australia.

Manly is another favorite. Lively surfing carnivals are among the highlights of the Sydney season, from November to March.

Boating. Sydney's prime yacht clubs are the Royal Sydney and the Cruising Yacht Club. Sailing and powerboats can be chartered, with or without a professional skipper. Inland, you can command a houseboat on the relaxing Hawkesbury River.

Fishing. For information about deep-sea expeditions from Sydney, check with the Sydney Game Fishing Club at Watsons Bay, Tel. 9337-5687. For outstanding trout fishing, the icy rivers of the Snowy Mountains are renowned. Details from Tourism New South Wales, Tel. 132-077.

Climbing new heights. The latest Sydney thrill is **BridgeClimb**, guided walks for small groups over the massive arches of Sydney Harbour Bridge. For decades, groups of daredevils have been doing this illicitly. Since this legal option was first offered in 1998, the waiting list has grown quite long, so if you're interested, it pays to book your climb as far in advance as you can.

It's not a cheap thrill—expect to pay about A$100. Climbers must be over 12 and physically fit, and those under 16 must be accompanied by an adult. You will be supplied with a special "bridgesuit," which you wear over your clothing, along with communications equipment and a harness linked to a static line. Avoid alcohol. Every climber must pass the same breath test that the police administer at random to drivers on NSW roads. All items that might drop must be left behind; unfortunately that includes cameras, though you will be given a complimentary photo of your group.

The walk extends for about 1,500 m (a little less than a mile) and reaches the very top of the bridge, 150 m (492 ft) above sea level. There are catwalks with handrails for support on most sections. BridgeClimb operates in all weathers "with the exception of electrical storms" (good thinking!).

The climb departs from 5 Cumberland Street, The Rocks. For bookings and information, Tel. (02) 9252-0077.

Spectator Sports

Football. Several types of football—commonly referred to as "footy"—are popular. Rugby Union, with teams of 15, is fast, rough, and engrossing to fans. Rugby League, the professional, international version, is the main event in Sydney. It offers tough physical challenges to players, 13 to a side. Australian Rules Football combines elements of rugby and Gaelic football. Look for long-distance kicks and passes and high scoring on an oversized, circular field with four goalposts, and 18 players on each side.

Cricket. Cricket is an Australian passion, and the country has produced some of the world's greatest players, including Sir Donald Bradman. The game is played in two forms—the classical, white-flannel style, which continues over a number of days—or one-day matches, with teams wearing bright colors dueling in sudden-death playoffs. Kerry Packer, Australia's richest man, founded the latter sort of cricket in 1977. Purists prefer the old-fashioned Test matches, which draw thousands of fans to the Sydney Cricket Ground every summer.

Horse racing. The races in Sydney are a glorious spectacle. Bookies line up behind their tote-boards, each carrying a large, white doctor-style bag in which money is placed. Sydney has four courses: Canterbury Park, Rosehill Gardens, Warwick Farm, and Royal Randwick. The last is closest to the CBD. Races go on all year, on Wednesdays and Saturdays, and big carnivals are held in spring and autumn.

ENTERTAINMENT

The *Sydney Morning Herald* publishes lift-out arts and music guide on Friday and an entertainment section on Saturday;

Sydneysiders love nothing more than a gamble, especially when it's as thrilling to watch as to win.

these list most arts and musical events for the coming week. Free weekly guides detailing alternative music and dance attractions are available at many inner-city pubs and bookshops.

Theater. Sydney has a flourishing theater scene covering mainstream and alternative productions. Big musicals and shows are staged at venues like the recently refurbished **State Theatre** (worth visiting for its over-the-top 1929 Rococo-revival decor) or the **Capitol Theatre**. Other establishments to look out for include the Belvoir Street Theatre (Oscar-winning actor Geoffrey Rush is a founder and director here), Bell Shakespeare Company, Ensemble Theatre, Lookout Theatre Club, New Theatre, and Stables Theatre. Not to forget the Sydney Opera House and the Harold Park Hotel, the latter being the haunt of stand-up comedians and

Dramatic silhouettes at dusk: the Opera House looks spectacular from any angle and at any time of day.

literary types. Reservations for many performances can be made by phone (see page 125).

Opera. The **Australian Opera**, based in Sydney, performs at the Sydney Opera House nine months of the year (January, February, and part of March, and from June to November).

Dance. The **Australian Ballet**, founded in 1962, is headquartered in Melbourne but spends nearly half its time performing in Sydney. **Sydney Dance Company** (two seasons a year) and **Dance Exchange** rank among the city's foremost modern dance troupes. Aboriginal groups such as **Bangarra Dance Theatre** and **Aboriginal Island Dance Theatre** perform in a variety of different venues.

Concerts. The concert hall of the **Sydney Opera House**, **Town Hall**, and the **Conservatorium of Music** are the main venues for serious music.

Jazz, blues, and rock. Bands with such bizarre names as Voodoo Underpants and Vicious Hairy Mary play at pubs and clubs all over the city. Popular venues include **Selina's** at Coogee Bay, the **Metro** in the CBD, the **Enmore Theatre** in Newtown and, for big gigs, the **Hordern Pavilion** in Moore Park or the **Sydney Entertainment Centre**. The **Basement in Reiby Place** near Circular Quay is known for its jazz; reservations are essential. On Friday, Saturday, and Sunday, blues bands play at the **Harbour View Hotel** in Lower Fort Street in the Rocks, underneath the bridge at the top of George Street.

Retro or tribute bands that impersonate other more famous groups are quite popular. Recent ones have included the Australian Queen Show, the ZZ Top Show, Bjorn Again (Abba clones), the Australian Jimmy Hendrix Tribute, and the Australian Madonna Show.

NIGHTLIFE

The list is endless and the variety dazzling. Everything from dance parties to all-night pubs where you can drink and play pool until sunrise and then leap into the surf. Posters slapped on walls and telegraph poles in the inner suburbs announce dance parties, gigs, plays, and concerts.

Sydney nightspots come and go. One of the oddest is **Kinselas** on Oxford Street's Taylor Square, currently under renovation. For many years it was a funeral parlor. Then it was a cabaret theater and dance hall, with patrons slurping martinis in the former embalming rooms.

Cinema. Multi-screen cinemas complexes vie with amusement arcades in downtown **George Street**. Specialized cinemas such as Paddington's **Academy Twin** and Glebe's **Valhalla** screen art films, first-run foreign films, and revivals.

A bold new casino. The **Star City** casino complex is set on a site about the size of seven football fields, just around the corner from Darling Harbour and not far from the National Maritime Museum. Surprisingly, Sydney was the last major

Australian city to get a casino. For decades, the only casino-style gambling took place in illegal gambling dens. Police frequently raided these, but mysterious tip-offs always allowed the king-pins to escape.

Sydney's casino has some typical Aussie touches, such as two vast cylindrical aquariums holding about 800 tropical fish and designed to impart a Great Barrier Reef feel. Another area is based on the Outback, with a replica of the Wave Wall (an outback landmark in Western Australia) and a recreated Outback hotel. Australia's own gambling game of two-up (which is played with two coins and goes back to convict times) is played in a Two-up Pit, styled on a hotel in the Kalgoorlie goldfields. You can participate or just sit in the bar and watch.

Quite apart from gambling, Star City offers all sorts of entertainment. Its 2,000-seat Lyric Theatre features top stage productions and its 1,000-seat showroom presents international and local cabaret acts.

Fox studios. The decision to give the Royal Agricultural Society's historic showground next to Centennial Park to Rupert Murdoch's Fox Group was controversial (for one thing, the famous Royal Easter Show had been held at the site since 1882). The redeveloped site includes a professional movie studio; *Babe: Pig in the City* was filmed here, and the final two episodes of the epic *Star Wars* saga are to be shot here in 2000.

At press time, a huge entertainment precinct, with 16 cinemas, retail outlets, cafés, and restaurants, was due to open in late 1999. Another big public area, The Fox Studios Backlot, will present experiences designed to involve audiences in cinema and television production.

Sydney Festival

Sydney Festival happens in January. This multi-media happening aims to present a world of entertainment in three weeks of sensational theater, dance, music, outdoor exhibitions, and visual arts, culminating on Australia Day, January 26. The Opera House is illuminated in a different festival theme color each year. International opera stars, avant-garde theater companies, open-air cinema, circuses, and Gypsy dancers and the like join forces with local acts to enthral crowds at various venues throughout the city. The Domain hosts huge open-air jazz or symphonic music concerts on Saturday nights.

The **Sydney Fringe Festival** runs alongside the main event, offerings include mixed male and female Nude Night Surfing at Bondi Beach, watched by 9,000 enthusiastic spectators in January 1999.

Calendar of Events

January	Sydney Festival
	Manly Surf Carnival
	Australia Day (Jan 26)
February	Gay & Lesbian Mardi Gras
	Fosters Tamworth Country Music Festival
March/April	Royal Easter Show, Homebush Bay
	ANZAC Day Parade (Apr 25)
May	Sydney Jazz Week
June	Manly Food and Wine Festival
	Sydney Film Festival
July	International Boat Show
	Yulefest, Blue Mountains
August	City to Surf Fun Run
September	Festival of the Winds, Bondi Beach
	Australian Open Tennis Championships
October	1000 Motor Race, Bathurst
	Manly Jazz Festival
	Hunter Valley Wine Festival
November	Horse of the Year Show
December	Sydney to Hobart Yacht Race
	(starts Dec 26)

Darling Harbour Monorail; aesthetic purists call it the "Monsterail" but children love it.

CHILDREN

Sydney has many activities to offer that will appeal to even the most demanding of children. Conveniently, three of the leading attractions are located in Darling Harbour: the **Monorail** (kids love it); **Tumbalong Park**; and **Sega World Sydney** with its nine major rides and 200 audio-visual arcade games. The "Search and Discover" section on the second floor of the **Australian Museum** lets children get their hands on all sorts of exciting exhibits that most museums would keep out of bounds. The **Powerhouse Museum** is full of big machines that exude endless kiddie appeal. The **Opera House** runs children's events such as the Babies Proms, which allows toddlers to get close to the musical instruments (Tel. 9250-7111). The **Art Gallery of New South Wales** holds special family events on Sundays, such as renditions of Aboriginal Dreamtime stories (Tel. 9225-1700).

EATING OUT

What to Eat and Drink

Modern Australian cuisine—sometimes called "Mod Oz"—takes fresh, high-quality ingredients and combines them with culinary approaches and techniques borrowed from all over the world. In the words of US food writer and cookbook author Barbara Kafka, "Australians have one of the most extraordinary assortments of basic ingredients of high quality anywhere in the world, and at exceptionally modest prices."

Immigrants, particularly Italians, have helped revolutionize the urban Sydney diet, moving it in a single generation from basic meat-and-veg fodder to what has been described as fusion food (a collage of culinary influences encompassing Asian, Mediterranean, maybe even a touch of Moroccan). Australian chefs have propelled the national taste buds into uncharted waters, experimenting widely and mixing the cuisines of Asia and Europe.

In 1996, Robert Carrier, the renowned cookbook author and television chef, visited Australia to judge the annual Remy Martin Cognac/Australian Gourmet Traveller Restaurant of the Year Award. "I've never had such tastes, such subtleties, such delights, such form, such color," he enthused. He concluded there were at least six restaurateurs in Sydney, who, if they set up in Paris, would be instant successes.

Chefs here have the advantage of being able to work with superb raw materials. Australia's size and climatic diversity make it possible to produce an astonishing variety of fruits and vegetables—apples, lychees, mandarins, custard apples, mangoes, strawberries, blackberries, passionfruit, and bok choy—to name just a few. A lot of these ingredients are seasonal and have to be freighted long distances, of course, so

Patrons study an array of delectable offerings at a Bondi cafe-deli.

the situation isn't quite perfect (it's not always possible, for instance, to buy a crisp, fresh apple in Sydney), but chefs never have to look too far to find ingredients that combine to produce astounding results that would be hard to duplicate anywhere else in the world.

And the good news is it doesn't have to cost a lot to eat well. Moderately priced restaurants abound in Sydney, especially in the inner suburbs. So-called Leagues Clubs (where poker-machine takings subsidize the kitchens) serve meals for just a few dollars, and the same is true of many pubs.

Bush Tucker

Over the past decade, Australian chefs have started using more and more native foods. Mysterious ingredients like muntari berries, bush tomatoes, Illawarra plums, lemon myrtle, and lilli pillies have begun to appear on restaurant menus, often blended with traditional dishes of meat and fish. This native food of Australia—the fruits, seeds, nuts, fungi, mammals, reptiles, fish, and birds that sustained Aborigines for tens of thousands of years—is referred to collectively as "bush tucker." Popular ingredients include quandongs (similar to a peach but with a rhubarb-like tang), wattle seeds (sometimes used in ice cream), Kakadu plums (less sweet than the usual variety), and bunya bunya nuts (delicious in satay sauces). Kangaroo and emu (a relative of the ostrich) have also found their way onto many menus;

Georgian Habits

Prolific Australian writer Thomas Keneally, author of *Schindler's Ark* (the basis of Steven Spielberg's movie *Schindler's List*), argues that Australians have remained essentially Georgian in character. Keneally draws a number of parallels between Georgian England and the contemporary Australian ethos: among them are a "a frenzy for gaming and gambling," a combination of rebelliousness and conservatism, and a respect for alcoholic consumption.

The wild rum-drinking of the young colony has abated and Aussies have switched to beer or wine. In 1997, Australians come fifth in the world beer-consumption league at 93.26 liters (197 US pints) a head, a drop of 5.83 liters (12.3 US pints) since 1993. Ahead of Australia (in order) were the Czech Republic, Germany, Belgium, and Britain. Following Australia came the US, Netherlands, Spain, Hungary, and Colombia.

Australians drink almost four times more beer than the world average. A health report released in 1999 revealed that the average Australian 12-year-old boy downs 3.5 alcoholic drinks a week and the average girl of the same age drinks 2.3 alcoholic drinks a week.

both are now commercially farmed and are low in fat and high in fiber. Two Aboriginal foods that have yet to become popular in Sydney restaurants are witchetty grubs (large grubs found in the trunks and roots of wattle trees) and bogong moths (a hefty migratory moth, usually roasted in a fire and eaten like peanuts).

Australian Wines

Australian wines are among the world's best—a judgment confirmed regularly at international wine shows. The Australian wine industry is aiming to become the world's most profitable and influential supplier of branded wines within 30 years, a target that assumes a massive increase in the value of Australia's wine exports. In 1997, at *Wine* magazine's International Wine Challenge, held in conjunction with the London Wine Trade Fair, an Australian wine was judged Best Red Wine of the Year and a leading Australian winemaker was named International Red Winemaker of the Year. White wines also do hold their own, with semillon/sauvignon blanc being a popular blend.

Many Sydney restaurants are BYO (bring your own), but wine and liquor stores are not hard to find and most offer a wide selection at very moderate prices. A number of the fully licensed restaurants have very well chosen wine cellars (see page 138).

The Amber Nectar

Beer in Australia is served cold, sometimes very cold. Australia's best-known beer is probably Fosters lager, but there are many more. Reschs, Tooheys, and VB (Victorian Bitter) are big-selling brands in Sydney bars. Some beers are sold in "new" and "old" varieties, the first being lager, the latter darker in color. Australia's standard alcoholic strength for draft beer is 4.9%. By contrast, the US standard is 3.5%. The word "light" (or "lite"), when applied to beer in Australia, means lighter in alcohol, not lighter in calories. The alcoholic strength of a beer must by law be displayed on the can or bottle.

"Boutique" beers, brewed in smaller batches, are popular in inner Sydney. Hahn is a good example. Coopers Ale, brewed in South Australia, has a loyal following. Coopers is more like a British beer (but colder!), and pretty strong at 5.8% alcohol.

A 285 ml (10-ounce) beer glass is called a "middie" in New South Wales and a 425 ml (15-ounce) glass is called a "schooner." A small bottle of beer is known throughout Australia as a "stubbie." A

Fine wines, Barossa Valley. If Bacchus were alive he'd be only too happy in Australia.

liquor store is called a bottle shop, or "bottle-o." To "shout" someone a drink means to buy them one, as in, "Can I shout you a drink?" Pub patrons may be "in a shout," which means they are with a group of drinkers who take turns to buy drinks for the whole group.

Where to Eat

Some of Sydney's most acclaimed restaurants are to be found in the Rocks, around Circular Quay, downtown, and at Darling Harbour. Don't limit your dining to these areas, though, because many other neighborhoods and nearby suburbs such as Kings Cross, Darlinghurst, Paddington, and Newtown offer exciting options as well. Oxford Street in Darlinghurst, for example (just a short ride from Circular Quay on CityRail), is lined with smaller restaurants, many of which offer outstanding Asian cuisine and seafood at moderate prices. The largest concentration is in the block immediately east of Taylor Square; really more of a crossroads than a square, the neighborhood is a bit scruffy, but the restaurants are great.

Crown Street, which heads off Oxford Street a block west of Taylor Square, is increasingly trendy. Here you'll find fine pub-restaurants like the Dolphin, the Clock, and a curious

and highly fashionable eatery called MG Café, where diners enjoy their meals in a sports car showroom.

A short stroll to the south on Crown Street takes you to Surry Hills, which boasts (at last count) three Japanese restaurants, four Turkish pide (pizza) houses, several Indian restaurants, a gourmet wood-fired pizza outlet, two or three Thai restaurants, and Georgio's, a coffee bar with an Italian name, owned by a Greek, and run by a Glaswegian. Around the corner in Cleveland Street (towards the corner of Elizabeth

Street) is a cluster of good-value Lebanese restaurants.

Others areas worth exploring when you're hungry include Kings Cross, which is peppered with stylish restaurants and funky cafés, particularly along Victoria Street; East Sydney near the Central Business District, noted for its Italian and Mod Oz eateries; and the western suburb of Newtown, which may have the largest concentration of ethnic restaurants in Sydney, everything from Greek, Italian, and Chinese to Turkish, Mongolian, and Thai. Bondi Beach to the south is

Beat this view: Sydney has no shortage of spots where you can eat while drinking in the beauty of the harbor.

renowned for its a profusion of seafood restaurants. On the North Shore, McMahon's Point and Crows Nest are the best bets.

Sydney Fish Market

Sydney's bustling fish market, on Blackwattle Bay in Pyrmont (just west of Darling Harbour), is worth a visit. Australian tuna, Tasmanian salmon, and blue swimmer crabs are air-freighted from here direct to Japan, where they appear on the auction block at Tokyo's Tsukiji Market not long after they are hauled from the sea. But much of the daily catch stays right in Sydney, to be sold at the market's daily early-morning auction (wholesale only) or throughout the day at the many retail outlets that line the wharf. You can easily put together a fine seafood meal by grazing your way past the sushi bars, fish cafés, and vendors offering everything from fresh, ice-cold raw oysters to grilled mixed-seafood platter (prepared al fresco). One of the best value lunches is the simplest. Just ask for a kilo (2.2 pounds) of large cooked prawns (shrimps) and pick a bottle of crisp white wine. Grab a seat at one of the tables on the dock and savor your meal while boats bob at anchor and pelicans soar overhead.

There are few places in the world where you'll be able to see as many varieties of freshwater fish, saltwater fish, and shellfish amassed in one place. The displays are overwhelming and many visitors find it hard to choose. Be adventurous and try something new, like "bugs," for example. Balmain bugs are a type of saltwater crustacean, similar to crayfish; they're highly favored by Sydneysiders. Other popular choices are yabbies (native freshwater crayfish), Tasmanian lobsters, baby octopus, freshwater barramundi, and King prawns (shrimp). You might even come across crocodile fillets from Darwin.

You can easily walk to the fish market from Darling Harbour. A pleasant alternative is to hop on one of the trains of the new Light Rail system, which runs from Central Station.

INDEX

HANDY TRAVEL TIPS

An A–Z Summary of Practical Information

A Accommodations 106
Airports 106
B Bicycle Rental 107
Budgeting for Your
Trip 107
C Camping 108
Car Rental 108
Climate 109
Clothing 110
Complaints 110
Crime and Safety 110
Customs and Entry/
Exit Formalities 111
D Driving 112
E Electricity 114
Embassies,
Consulates, High
Commissions 114
Emergencies 115
G Gay and Lesbian
Travelers 115
Getting to Sydney 116
Guides and Tours 116
H Health and Medical
Care 116
Hitchhiking 118
Holidays 118
L Language 118
Laundry and Dry
Cleaning 119
M Maps 119
Media 119
Money Matters 120
O Open Hours 121
P Police 121
Post Offices 122
Public Transportation
122
R Religion 124
T Telephones 124
Tickets 125
Time Zones 125
Tipping 126
Toilets 126
Tourist Information
Offices 126
W Weights and
Measures 127
Y Youth Hostels 128

Sydney

A

ACCOMMODATIONS (See also CAMPING and YOUTH HOSTELS)

Sydney's hotel-room inventory rose rapidly in the run up to the Olympics, causing average room rates to stall and even fall. Hotel chains with lodgings in the city include Accor Asia Pacific, Southern Pacific Hotels Corporation (SPHC), the Australian-based Rydges Hotels, Sheraton, Hyatt International, Hilton International, Regent International, and the Japanese groups ANA and Nikko. Large five-star hotels in downtown include the Regent, the ANA, the Sheraton on the Park, the Ritz-Carlton, the Hilton, and the Wentworth (a Rydges property).

Overseas offices of the Australian Tourist Commission have listings of hotels and motels. You can reserve accommodations through your travel agent or airline. Within Australia, book through the state tourist offices, domestic airlines, and hotel chains. Accommodations may be harder to find when Australians themselves go traveling, during the school holidays. These are staggered state by state except for the year-end period (December–February) when schools everywhere close. Australian Tourist Commission offices can provide details (see TOURIST INFORMATION).

AIRPORTS

Sydney Airport, about 10 km (6 miles) from the city center, is Australia's busiest international airport. It has been upgraded over the last few years to offer more shops, restaurants, bars, and open space. A rail link between the airport and Sydney's Central Station is due to open in May 2000, about three months before the Olympic Games. The 10-km rail line will have five stations, including one at Sydney Airport's international terminal and another at the domestic terminal. A new freeway linking downtown Sydney with the airport is due for completion in January 2000, and a new elevated road to the domestic terminal should improve road traffic flows in and around the airport by doubling current road capacity.

Arriving passengers can travel from Sydney Airport to town by taxi (10–20 minutes) or bus (20–30 minutes). The airport bus service goes to the door of major hotels. Note that the domestic and international terminals are a shuttle-bus ride apart.

Other principal international gateways in Australia are Melbourne, Brisbane, Cairns, Darwin, and Perth; connecting flights are available from Sydney and these cities to airports in Adelaide, Hobart, and Townsville.

 B

BICYCLE RENTAL

Most Australian cities are reasonably attuned to cyclists. Cars clog Sydney's roads, however, and attempts by the traffic authorities to cater to Sydney's sizable cycling fraternity have often resulted in little more than cosmetic changes. Bicycle lanes are marked on some inner-city roads, but most drivers ignore them. Many drain covers have slots that run parallel to the curb, so cycle carefully! You can rent a bike in Sydney or the suburbs, or sign up for a tour that includes transport to and from a scenic area (bikes provided), food, and accommodation. Cyclists must by law wear helmets. Bicycle New South Wales has information and literature, Tel. (02) 9283-5200.

BUDGETING for YOUR TRIP

Inflation in Australia was low throughout the 1990s, and the basics—food, accommodations, admission charges—are still comparatively inexpensive. A plate of noodles or pasta in an average restaurant costs about $8. A bottle of Australian wine from a liquor store starts at about $8, a 260 ml glass of beer (almost one US pint) in a pub cost from $A2.50, and a cup of coffee or tea costs about $A2. Entry to a museum or art gallery ranges from free up to $A12 per person.

Things may be changing, however. The government of Prime Minister John Howard has declared its intention to place a 10% VAT-style tax on all goods and services, including food. This tax, due to take force in 2000, will raise many prices.

Transportation costs. Air travel is a relatively high-ticket item, but international passengers may be entitled to discounted travel within Australia, depending on the airline they arrived on and the type of fare. International fares to and within Australia have fallen steadily in real terms over the past decade. On the ground, train travel can be competitive for shorter distances. Countrylink, the NSW State Rail service, offers an adult economy return trip from Sydney to Canberra for about $80, for a distance of about 560 km (350 miles). The approximate cost of a half-day coach sightseeing tour is $A36–$A50 per person. A Great Barrier Reef cruise runs from $A50 to $A150 per person. In early 1999, gasoline (petrol) costs about A$0.80 a liter, more expensive than in the US but cheaper than in most European countries. Renting a small car cost from $A45 per day and renting a camper van (sleeping two) cost about $A100 per day. Caravan park sites often charged less than A$15 a night.

Accommodations. A room at a backpacker hostel runs from $A15 to $A20 per night. Rooms at five-star hotels start at $A250 per night. Sydney has a range of lodging options in between (see RECOMMENDED HOTELS on page 129). The NSW State Government applies a bed tax of 10% on Sydney hotels, but it only affects downtown hotels—not those in, say, Bondi.

C

CAMPING

Australians are avid campers, and you'll find campsites all over the country. The sites tend to be packed during school holidays. They all have at least the basic amenities, and in some cases much more in the way of comfort. Aside from roomy tents with lights and floors, some installations have caravans (trailers) or cabins. Showers, toilets, laundry facilities, and barbecue grills are commonly available. Sheets and blankets can often be hired. The national parks generally have well-organized camping facilities. To camp beyond the designated zone you must ask rangers for permission. The Basin scenic campsite on the shore of Pittwater in Ku-Ring-Gai Chase National Park, quite close to the city, is a favorite. Many coach tours include camping segments, or you can hire a camper van or motor home by the day or week (see CAR RENTAL).

CAR RENTAL

In inner-city Sydney, with its traffic jams and parking hassles, a car is a burden. To see the Australian countryside at your own pace, however, there's no substitute for a car or a four-wheel-drive vehicle. Brisk competition among international and local car rental companies means you can often find economical rates or special deals. Unlimited mileage is common, and there are often weekend discounts. If you announce that you intend to drive in remote country areas, rates may be considerably higher. In general, it's worth shopping around. But be careful—some companies impose a metropolitan limit on vehicles. Check first, as your insurance won't be valid outside the designated area.

To rent a car you'll need a current Australian, overseas, or International Driver's License. The minimum age is 21, or in some cases 25. Third-party insurance is automatically included; for an additional fee you can also sign up for collision damage and personal accident insurance.

You can pick up a car in one city and return it elsewhere. Interstate arrangements are commonly available from the big firms like Avis, Hertz, Thrifty, and Budget, which also have offices at airports. Camper vans and caravans (trailers) are available, though many are reserved far in advance for school holiday periods.

CLIMATE

Sydney enjoys a temperate and pleasant climate. It's not perfect; the downside is late-summer humidity, which runs at an average 69% and makes Sydney the most humid Australian city outside tropical Darwin in the far north. Ocean breezes help cool Sydney's coastal suburbs. February and March are sultry months, ideal for mosquitoes, which are a nuisance in some suburbs but not a health threat.

Rain tends to fall in intense, tropical bursts. Seasons are the reverse of those in the northern hemisphere, with winter running from June to August. April and May are pleasant months, resembling European springtime. Sydney never receives a long twilight, even in midsummer. The NSW Outback is mostly very hot from December to February. For your general guidance, here are some average daily maximum and minimum Sydney temperatures, month by month:

	J	F	M	A	M	J	J	A	S	O	N	D
Max °C	26	26	25	22	19	17	16	18	20	22	24	25
Min °C	18	19	17	15	11	9	8	9	11	13	15	17
Max °F	79	79	77	72	66	63	61	64	68	72	75	77
Min °F	64	66	63	59	52	48	46	48	52	55	59	63

Sydney

Ocean temperature

°C	22	22	22	21	14	17	16	16	16	17	19	20
°F	72	72	72	70	58	63	61	61	61	63	66	68

Average number of days of traceable rainfall

14	13	14	14	13	12	12	11	12	12	12	13

CLOTHING

Whatever your itinerary, whatever the season, forget an overcoat. A sweater may come in handy, however, even in summer when, after a hot day in the sun, the evening breeze can seem chilly. A light raincoat will serve in almost any season. Anywhere you go you'll need comfortable walking shoes. While Sydneysiders dress casually at weekends (shorts, a short-sleeved shirt or T-shirt, and sneakers or sandals are perfect), business attire can be surprisingly conservative. Sydney has yet to adapt fully to its climate and adopt the open-necked informality seen in countries like Israel or the Philippines.

Restaurants have dropped the requirement for men to wear jacket and tie, but some establishments may refuse customers wearing T-shirts, tank tops, or ripped jeans. Entering clubs generally requires a collared shirt and covered shoes—not sneakers or sandals.

COMPLAINTS

If you think you've been overcharged or unfairly dealt with, the personal approach can be effective in plain-talking Australia. If not, the NSW Department of Fair Trading may help. Tel. (02) 9286-0006.

CRIME and SAFETY

Sydney's murder rate (two per each 100,000 citizens) is low by world standards and the city is generally safe. It's still wise to take precautions against burglary and petty theft. Place your valuables in a hotel's safe deposit box or in-room safe. Lock your room and your car. Be on the alert for pickpockets on crowded buses and in markets.

Muggings and fights sometimes happen. It's better to avoid Hyde Park after dark, particularly if on your own. William Street, which runs from Hyde Park to Kings Cross, is another place where it's unwise to loiter after dark. The secluded back streets of Kings Cross have a similar reputation, although the main strip is safe enough. Police report instances of bag snatching and fights around the Redfern Station and Waterloo areas in inner-southern Sydney.

CUSTOMS and ENTRY and EXIT FORMALITIES

Australia requires all visitors to hold a visa. Travel industry groups lobby constantly against this archaic regulation, but so far without success. Citizens of New Zealand (which enjoys strong historical links with Australia) receive an automatic electronic visa when they present their passports at the Immigration counter.

Australia's new Electronic Travel Authority (ETA) allows travel agents to issue an "invisible visa" electronically to visitors at time of booking in their home countries. This has greatly shortened the time most passengers have to wait at Sydney Airport's Customs and Immigration counter. It's now down to less than a minute each, on average.

The ETA eliminates having to find an embassy or consulate. There is no more form filling or standing in line—just a 10-second electronic transaction after passport data is keyed in by the travel agent. The process can be completed in person or over the phone. Tourists or travelers visiting friends or relatives and wishing to stay for up to three months on each visit within a 12-month period should apply for the free Tourist ETA (Type V). Those making a business visit should inquire whether they require a type BL or type BS visa.

If you wish to extend your stay beyond three months, you will need to contact the nearest office of the Department of Immigration and Multicultural Affairs in Australia before the end of your three-month stay period.

Australia operates reciprocal working holiday schemes with Canada, Ireland, Japan, Korea, Malta, the Netherlands, and the UK, for applicants between 18 and 25 (and in special circumstances, 26 to 30), either single or married without children. Working holiday visas allow recipients to work for up to three months at a time, over a one-year period.

Entry formalities. On the last leg of your flight to Australia you'll be asked to complete a customs form, swearing that you are not trying to import foreign foodstuffs, weapons, drugs, or other forbidden articles. There is also an Immigration form. Vaccinations are not required unless you have come from or visited a yellow fever–infected country or zone within six days prior to arrival. You may be required to show your return or onward ticket, and you may need to prove that your funds are sufficient to last out your planned stay.

Exit formalities. Departure tax is now built into air tickets (a measure imposed over much protest from airlines). You'll need to fill out a departure form for the Immigration authorities. If you are carrying A$10,000 or more in foreign currency, you must declare it to Customs.

Duty-free. Anyone over the age of 18 is allowed to bring into Australia $A400 worth of goods not including alcohol or tobacco; 1,125 ml (about 1.6 US pints) of alcohol (including wine, beer, or spirits); and 250 cigarettes or 250 grams of cigars or tobacco products other than cigarettes.

DRIVING

Like Britain, New Zealand, Japan, and many Asian countries, Australia drives on the left—which means the steering wheel is on the right and you pass on the right. Australian roads are good considering the size of the country and the challenges of distance, terrain, and climate. Freeways link populous regions, but most country roads are two-lane highways, which can be crowded at busy times.

Regulations. Drivers and passengers must wear seat belts. (The exception is motor coaches, although many of them feature seat belts as an option). Car-rental companies can supply suitable child restraints, boosters, and baby capsules and seats, at an extra charge. A tourist may drive in Australia on a valid overseas license for the same class of vehicle. Licenses must be carried when driving. If the license is in a language other than English, the visitor must carry a translation with the license. An International Drivers Permit is not sufficient by itself and must be accompanied by a valid drivers permit.

The speed limit in cities is generally 60 km/h (about 35 mph), but on suburban streets it sometimes is cut to 40 km/h (about 25 mph). In the NSW countryside, the limit is 110km/h (about 70 mph). Police make random checks for drugs or drink, using breath tests. The limit on alcohol in the blood is 0.05, meaning in practice that three glasses of wine or three medium-size ("middy") glasses of beer in an hour will take you to the limit. If you are under 25 and in your first three years of driving, you must be under 0.02, which doesn't allow you to drink at all.

City driving. Heavy traffic and parking problems afflict the downtown area, which might explain why Sydney drivers are so impatient and why they tend (when road conditions permit) to drive too fast. Parking meters and "no standing" zones proliferate.

Outback driving. Thoroughly check the condition of your car and be sure you have a spare wheel and plenty of spare drinking water. Find out about the fuel situation in advance and always leave word as to your destination and anticipated arrival time. Fill up the fuel tank at every opportunity, for the next station may be a few hundred kilometers away. Some dirt roads are so smooth you may be tempted to speed, but conditions can change abruptly. Be cautious with road trains, consisting of three or four huge trailers barreling down the highway towed by a high-powered truck. Pass one, if you dare, with the greatest of care.

Fuel. Many filling stations are open only during normal shopping hours, so you may have to ask where out-of-hours service is available. Gasoline (petrol) in Australia comes in super, leaded, unleaded regular, and premium unleaded grades and is sold by the liter. In early 1999 it cost between A$0.70 and A$0.80 a liter, with unleaded petrol 2¢ less per liter than leaded petrol. Prices are often higher in country areas. Most stations are self-service and accept international credit cards.

Road signs. Signs are generally good, especially along heavily used roads. All distances are measured in kilometers. White-on-brown direction signs signal tourist attractions and natural wonders. To drive into the center of any city, simply follow the signs marked "City." Leaving a city is less straightforward: exit routes are often signposted with the assumption that every driver has local experience, so you may need a good map and some advance planning. Most road signs are the standard international pictographs, but some are unique to Australia, such as large silhouette images of kangaroos or wombats, warning that you may encounter these animals crossing the road. Some signs use words, such as:

Crest steep	Hilltop limiting visibility
Cyclist hazard	Dangerous for cyclists

Sydney

Dip	Severe depression in road surface
Hump	Bump or speed obstacle
Safety Ramp	Uphill escape lane from a steep downhill road
Soft Edges	Soft shoulders

Fluid measures

Distance

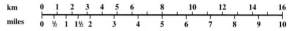

ELECTRICITY

The standard throughout Australia is 230–250 volt, 50-cycle AC. Three-pronged plugs, in the shape of a bird's footprint, are universal. They are the same as those used in New Zealand and many Pacific countries. If you're from anywhere else, you'll need an adapter. Many hotel rooms also have 110-volt outlets for razors and small appliances.

EMBASSIES, CONSULATES, HIGH COMMISSIONS

The embassies or high commissions of about 70 countries are established in Canberra, the national capital. They have consular sections dealing with passport renewal, visas, and other formalities. More than 40 countries also have diplomatic representation in Sydney.

Unless otherwise noted, the following list refers to consulates located in Sydney:

Canada: Level 5, Quay West Building, 111 Harrington Street; Tel.(02) 9364-3050

New Zealand: Level 14, Gold Fields Building, 1 Alfred Street, Circular Quay; Tel. (02) 9247-1999

South Africa (High Commission): Rhodes Place, State Circle, Yarralumla, Canberra, ACT 2600; Tel. (02) 6273-2424/2526

UK: Level 16, The Gateway, 1 Macquarie Place, Sydney Cove; Tel. (02) 9247-7521

US: Level 59, MLC Centre, 19-29 Martin Place; Tel. (02) 9373-9200

EMERGENCIES

For an ambulance, the fire department, or the police, dial **000**. This number is in service in all cities and towns, and no coin is required from public telephones. If you're in a remote area, look for the emergency numbers inside the front cover of the local telephone directory.

G

GAY and LESBIAN TRAVELERS

Sydney is one of the world's major gay cities, sometimes called "the Gay Capital of the Southern Hemisphere." It's certainly the gay and lesbian capital of Australia. Estimates of the gay population vary, but 400,000 is commonly quoted, which would make one Sydneysider in ten gay. NSW has outlawed vilification of gays, or discrimination against them, although intolerance still exists.

Sydney's gay population is big enough to sustain two free weekly publications, *Sydney Star Observer* and *Capital Q Weekly.* Obtainable from book shops, pubs, and cafés throughout inner Sydney, these contain news and information on gay events and venues.

Sydney's main gay precinct is Oxford Street (sometimes called "the Golden Mile") and the surrounding Darlinghurst area. Another neighborhood with a fairly strong gay scene is King Street in Newtown. Well-known pubs around Oxford Street favored by the gay male community include the Albury, the Beauchamp, and the Beresford. In Newtown, men congregate at the Imperial Hotel and the Newtown Hotel, while lesbians hang out at the Bank Hotel and Sirens.

Sydney

GETTING TO SYDNEY

By Air

Flights from Asia, North America, and Europe serve international airports around Australia, of which Sydney's is the busiest. Australia is included in several "round-the-world" fare schemes—arrangements between two or more airlines that allow passengers to travel globally at bargain rates, provided they complete their journeys within a year and travel in one direction only. One such fare, Global Explorer, combines the services of Qantas, British Airways, and American Airlines, covering more than 480 destinations worldwide. It costs something like six cents/km—cheaper than a bus fare. Flight times (approximate) are New York–Sydney, 22 hours; Los Angeles–Sydney, 15 hours; and London–Sydney, 21 hours. You can usually break the flight for a day or two at one of the stops along the way; in most cases this doesn't affect the price of the air ticket.

By Sea

A number of Australian ports, notably Sydney and Cairns, feature in the itineraries of cruise ships. You can fly to, say, Bali or Singapore and embark on the liner there, sail to Australia, then fly home from any Australian city, or resume the cruise at another port.

GUIDES and TOURS

Tour companies offer a broad choice of excursions, from half a day in Sydney to long-haul journeys into the Outback. Harbor cruises range from the general sightseeing tour to specialized visits to historic Fort Denison. There are also local walking tours—around The Rocks, for instance—and tours for cyclists, wildlife-lovers and others with special interests.

HEALTH and MEDICAL CARE

Standards of hygiene are high, particularly in food preparation. Doctors and dentists are proficient and hospitals well equipped. If you fall ill, your hotel can call a doctor or refer you to one, or you can ask your embassy, high commission, or consulate for a list of approved doctors. You should take out health insurance before departure to cover your stay in Australia. Also ensure you have personal insurance or travel insurance with a comprehensive health component to cover the possibility of illness or accident.

Medicare, Australia's national health insurance scheme, covers visitors from New Zealand, UK, Ireland, Malta, Sweden, Italy, Finland, and the Netherlands. To be eligible, contact your national health scheme before traveling to Australia to ensure you have the correct documents to enroll at any Medicare office on arrival in Australia. The agreement covers urgent treatment but not elective surgery, dental care, ambulance services, or illness arising en-route to Australia. The agreements do not cover repatriation in the case of serious illness or injury.

You are allowed to bring "reasonable quantities" of prescribed nonnarcotic medications. All should be clearly labeled and identifiable. For large quantities, bring a doctor's certificate to produce at Customs if necessary. All medication must be carried in personal hand luggage. Local pharmacies, called chemists, can fill most prescriptions—which must be written by an Australian-registered doctor.

Health hazards exist in the seas and the countryside. Ultraviolet levels are high and sunburn can be rapid; high-factor protective cream is essential if exposed, even on cloudy days. Farther afield, poisonous snakes and spiders lurk. You are unlikely to encounter snakes in central Sydney, but they sometimes crop up in the suburbs. Most dangerous are death adders. The Sydney funnelweb spider, dark and bulbous, is one of the world's most lethal. An antivenin has been developed. The spider lives in holes in the ground, chiefly in Sydney's northern suburbs. Bites are rare (about 10 victims a year) and require immediate medical attention. If you or someone you're traveling with is bitten, try to catch the spider for identification. Other poisonous spiders include the redback, the eastern mouse spider, and the white-tail. Bites from these are rare and seldom lethal, but see a doctor if bitten.

Shark attacks are extremely rare. In certain seasons and areas, bluebottles (dangerous jellyfish) may cluster. The sting is agonising but can be treated with vinegar. In the north of Australia, crocodiles can be a menace to swimmers. Obey the signs.

Some Sydney beaches have suffered sewage pollution problems. Beachwatch Infoline, Tel. (02) 9901-7996, gives daily updates. Sydney had two drinking water scares in 1998, when the microscopic parasites giardia and cryptosporidium turned up in the water supply. Health authorities advised people to boil drinking water for at least a minute. The bugs were eliminated from the water and an upgrade of the city's water infrastructure was announced. Water is now monitored daily.

Sydney has Australia's highest rate of AIDS-related deaths (seven per 100,000 people), so protect yourself from risks such as exposure to HIV and other sexually transmitted diseases.

HITCHHIKING

It's better not to. Hitchhiking is banned on freeways and throughout the whole state of Queensland. Even where it is tolerated, it can be risky, and tourism authorities strongly discourage it (some hitchhikers have disappeared without trace). Some city hostels feature notice boards where people driving interstate can advertise for a traveling companion to share costs. That way, you at least get to meet the person you might travel with. Cut-rate bus travel is a safer and better option.

HOLIDAYS

1 January	*New Year's Day*
26 January	*Australia Day*
March/April	*Good Friday, Holy Saturday, Easter Monday*
25 April	*Anzac Day (Australian and New Zealand Army Corps)*
June (2nd Monday)	*Queen's Birthday*
25 December	*Christmas Day*
26 December	*Boxing Day*

School holidays arrive four times a year, the longest one being in the summer through the latter part of December and all January.

LANGUAGE

Australian is spoken everywhere. The vernacular is sometimes called *Strine,* which is how the word "Australian" sounds in an extreme Australian pronunciation. Educated and cultivated Australians tend to speak in more neutral tones; Strine in the back blocks can sound to an American or European ear like a profound Cockney accent piped through the nose. Foreigners who listen carefully usually understand what's said, at least when it's repeated.

Special multicultural radio stations broadcast in more than 50 languages. Non-English speakers with problems can get help from the telephone Translating and Interpreting Service (TIS), which can translate vital phone calls. TIS—Tel. 131-450—operates round the clock in the bigger cities, for the price of a local phone call. Sometimes an interpreting charge or call charges may apply.

LAUNDRY and DRY CLEANING

Hotels and motels usually offer same-day laundry and dry-cleaning service for guests, though it tends to be quite expensive. Ask the receptionist, porter, or maid. Many hotels and motels also have do-it-yourself washers and dryers on the premises, as well as irons and ironing boards in the rooms.

M

MAPS

State and local tourist offices give away useful maps of their areas, and there are free specialized maps, of Darling Harbour, for instance, or the Sydney ferry network. Car hire companies often supply free city directories showing each street and place of interest. For more detailed maps, it may be worth buying a *Gregory's Street Directory* at a newsstand or bookstore.

MEDIA

Newspapers. Sydney's biggest-selling daily, the *Sydney Morning Herald,* publishes a TV guide on Mondays, a restaurant and cooking guide called Good Living on Tuesdays, and an entertainment guide called Metro on Fridays. Other daily papers are the *Daily Telegraph,* the *Australian,* and the *Australian Financial Review.* The latter two circulate nationally. Dozens of periodicals aimed at the immigrant communities are published in numerous languages. Specialist newsstands in Sydney sell newspapers airlifted from New York, London, Rome, Paris, Hong Kong, and Singapore.

Sydney

Television. Excluding pay TV, five channels are available: ABC (channel 2) is taxpayer-funded and commercial-free; Channel 9 has the highest ratings; others are Channels 7 and 10. Most interesting is SBS, which broadcasts foreign films with subtitles, documentaries, European sports, and news programs concentrating on overseas coverage.

Radio. AM stations include ABC Radio National (576AM), intelligent and articulate. ABC Parliamentary and News Network (630AM), concentrates on worldwide news. ABC 2BL (702AM) is most popular of the ABC (taxpayer funded) stations—good morning news and current affairs. 2UE (945AM) has much talkback. 2KY (1017AM) has a lot of horse racing. Others are 2GB (873AM) and 2CH (1170AM). SBS Radio (1386AM) broadcasts ethnic radio programs in their own languages. FM stations include Sydney Information Radio (87.8FM), broadcasting for tourists in the city area only. The best two classical music FM stations are 2MBS (102.5FM) and Classic FM (92.9FM). The best two popular music FM stations are Triple J (105.7FM) and MMM (104.9FM).

MONEY MATTERS

Currency. You don't have to reach for a credit card to use plastic in Australia—banknotes (bills) are made of it and feature transparent panels instead of watermarks. Australian currency is decimal-based, with the dollar as the basic unit (100 cents equals one dollar). Notes come in $100, $50, $20, $10, and $5 denominations. Coins come in 5c, 10c, 20c, 50c, $1, and $2 denominations. As for credit cards, American Express, Bankcard, MasterCard, Visa, and Diners Club are widely accepted, but you may encounter problems with them in smaller towns and country areas and small retail shops.

Currency exchange. All international airports in Australia provide currency exchange facilities, and foreign bills or travelers' checks can be converted at most banks. Cash travelers' checks at banks or larger hotels, as it may be difficult elsewhere. Some banks may charge a fee for cashing them—Australian banks charge for just about everything these days.

ATMs. ATM cards are widely used and machines are widespread. You may be able to obtain cash directly in this way using the same

PIN number you use at home, provided your card has been validated for international access. Electronic point-of-sale transactions (EFT-POS) are available at larger stores.

 O

OPEN HOURS

Banks. Generally open from 9:30am to 4pm Monday through Thursday and from 9:30am to 5pm on Fridays. Selected banking facilities my be available on Saturday morning, but don't bank on it. Currency exchange facilities at Sydney Airport are open all hours.

Post offices. Monday through Friday 9am–5pm. (See Post Offices for more information.)

Shops. The big department stores are open from 9am to 5.30pm Monday to Friday and from 9am to 4pm on Saturday. Thursday is late shopping night when stores stay open until 8 or 9pm. Stores in some suburbs are open late on other nights. Shopping centers like the Queen Victoria Building and Harbourside are open seven days a week.

Bars/pubs/hotels. Licensing hours vary, but a typical schedule would be 10am to 10pm or 11pm Monday to Saturday, with most pubs open by noon on Sundays as well. (Some pubs, such as the Crown on the corner of Cleveland and Crown streets, Surry Hills, never close.) Nightclubs can carry on until the following morning, if the clientelc can stand it.

 P

POLICE

Each state (and the Northern Territory) operates its own police force, covering both urban and rural areas. The Australian Federal Police, based in Canberra, has jurisdiction over government property, including airports. It deals with interstate problems like drugs and organized crime. Sydney police are generally helpful and friendly. The emergency number is 000.

Sydney

POST OFFICES

Australia's post offices are signposted "Australia Post." Most adhere to a 9am to 5pm schedule Monday to Friday, though Sydney's General Post Office (GPO) in Pitt Street near Martin Place is open 8:15am to 5:30pm Monday to Friday and 8:30am to noon Saturday. This is the main post office for post restante—take ID with you if picking some up.

Postcards to the US cost 95 cents, to Europe $1. Letters cost $1.05 and $1.20 respectively and international aerograms cost 70 cents, whatever their destination. Stamps are often available at front desks of hotels and motels and at some retail outlets. Mailboxes throughout Australia are red with an Australia Post logo. Most post offices have fax facilities, as do hotels. Internet cafes exist in a few places. There's one upstairs at the Hotel Sweeney in the CBD (corner of Clarence and Druitt streets) and there are several around Kings Cross. There's even one in the Australian Museum.

PUBLIC TRANSPORTATION

The number to call for information on Sydney's public ferries, buses, and trains is **131-500**.

Buses. Buses are a practical option during business hours, but service tapers off after dark. (The trains are faster, but they run underground in the city, so buses are better for sightseeing.) The two main starting points for buses are at Wynyard Park on York Street (for the northern suburbs) and at Circular Quay (all other directions). The fare depends on the distance traveled; tickets may be purchased from the driver or from bus company employees at the main stops. Bus route numbers starting with X are express services with limited stops.

Two bus services, red Sydney Explorer and blue Bondi and Bay Explorer, offer great sightseeing value. The first covers all the main central Sydney sights and the second visits the bays, beaches, and attractions of the eastern side of town, including Kings Cross and Watsons Bay. Pay the driver A$20 for a day ticket and you can hop on an off as you please. They run frequently. Sydney Passes are good value, offering unlimited rides on both the red and blue sight-seeing buses, plus access to the Airport Express bus, rail travel, and all ferry services; the passes are available in three-, five-, and seven-day versions.

Railway. Sydney's underground railway system (subway) operates from 4:30am to midnight; it's the central unit of a railway network that stretches out to the suburbs. After midnight, the Nightride bus service takes over and runs through the night. Sydney's trains are double-deck, and station platforms are marked with special "Night safe" areas, to show you which carriages are open (those next to the guard's compartment). Other carriages may be closed after dark.

Monorail. This links the central city and Darling Harbour. It shuts down at 9pm weekdays in winter, but runs til midnight in summer.

Ferries. A vital part of life in Sydney, with so many commuters continually criss-crossing the harbor, ferries sail between 6am and 11pm daily. Most depart from Circular Quay, providing inexpensive outings for sightseers to Kirribilli, Neutral Bay, or Taronga Zoo. Ferries or fast JetCats shuttle between Circular Quay and Manly. And the slow but scenic way from Circular Quay to Darling Harbour is by ferry. Water taxis let you set your own itinerary, but they are expensive. Tel. (02) 9810-5010 or (02) 9922-4252.

Taxis. Visitor complaints about cabs usually center on: (a) dirty cabs, (b) drivers who can't speak English, and (c) drivers who get lost. In 1998 the authorities acted, decreeing that all drivers must wear uniforms. This move didn't exactly solve the problem, and some drivers still ask their passengers, "How do you get there?" or stop their cabs to check a street map if heading for an unfamiliar destination. (If they stop to read a map, they must turn off the meter.)

That aside, most cabbies are competent. You can hail a cab on the street if the orange light on top is lit. Otherwise, go to one of the cab stands at shopping centers, transport terminals, or big hotels, and take the first taxi in the rank. Or phone for a taxi; Tel. 131-415 or 131-017. Meters indicate the fare plus any extras, such as waiting time. Australians usually sit next to the taxi driver, but if you prefer the back seat, no offense is taken. It is not customary to tip taxi drivers.

Light rail. Sydney was once second only to London in the size of its tramway system. Tramcars ran throughout the city to as far away as

Bondi Beach. Foolishly, however, Sydney scrapped its trams in the early 1960s. A new-style tram service, renamed "light rail," is now operating on one route. It costs considerably more per stop that the public railway, but is quite scenic, running from Central Station through Chinatown past Darling Harbour to the Fish Market and a little beyond.

R

RELIGION

The majority religion in Australia is Christianity. The number of Roman Catholics recently overtook the number of Anglicans (Church of England). Next comes the Uniting Church, Presbyterian, and Eastern Orthodox. Of the non-Christian faiths, Muslims are the largest group, followed by Jews and Buddhists. To find the church or temple of your choice, check at your hotel desk or look in the Yellow Pages of the telephone directory under "Churches and Synagogues."

T

TELEPHONES

Australia's country code is 61 and the code for Sydney is 2. To call a Sydney number from another country dial your own country's international access code, then 612, then the local Sydney phone number. Australia's telephone network, run by Telstra (which used to be called Telecom Australia) is sophisticated; you can dial anywhere in the country from almost any phone, even in the Outback, and expect a loud and clear line. Many hotel rooms have phones from which you can dial cross-country (STD) or internationally (IDD) (remember, though, that hotels often add hefty surcharges to your phone bill).

The minimum cost of a local public pay phone call is 40 cents. Long distance calls within Australia (STD) and International Direct Dialling (IDD) calls can be made on Telstra public pay phones. Check with the operator for these charges as they vary for distances and the time of day of the call. Public pay phones accept most coins as well as Phonecards—pre-paid cards used to make local, STD, and IDD calls on public phones. (Some public phones accept only

Phonecards.) Phonecards are widely sold at newsstands and other shops, and come in denominations of $5, $10, $20, and $50. The Telstra PhoneAway pre-paid card enables you to use virtually any phone in Australia—home and office phones, mobile phones, hotel and pay phones—all call costs are charged against the card. Credit phones, found at airports, many hotels, and several center-city locations, accept most major credit cards such as AMEX, MasterCard, and Visa. Country Direct is a service that lets you speak directly with an operator in your home country. Cash is not needed since the call is charged to the receiving number or to your telephone credit card. Country Direct calling guides are available through Telstra shops, travel agents, and tour operators.

Phone books give full instructions on dialing and details on emergency and other services. To reach an overseas number, dial 0011, then the country code of the destination, the area code, and the local number.

TICKETS

Tickets bought directly from the box office in advance are generally the cheapest. Alternatively, try one of the major booking agencies, FirstCall, Tel. (02) 9320-9000, or Ticketek, Tel. (02) 9260-0260. Or try your luck at the Halftix booth, which sells cutrate tickets for the same evening's performances (though not for all shows). The Halftix booth's location at Martin Place was under threat at time of writing; call 1900-926-655 to find out where the booth is and what it's offering.

TIME ZONES

Australia has three time zones: Australian Eastern Standard Time (EST), which operates in New South Wales, Australian Capital Territory, Queensland, Victoria, and Tasmania; Central Standard Time (CST) in South Australia and the Northern Territory; and Western Standard Time (WST) in Western Australia. CST is 30 minutes behind EST, while WST is two hours behind EST. Daylight saving (clocks forward an hour) runs in New South Wales, the Australian Capital Territory (Canberra and surrounds), Victoria, and South Australia from the end of October to the end of March, and in Tasmania from the beginning of October through March. The Northern Territory, Western Australia, and Queensland do not apply daylight saving time during the summer.

Sydney is on EST, which is 10 hours ahead of Greenwich Mean Time, 15 hours ahead of New York, and 18 hours ahead of California.

TIPPING

Tipping is a relatively recent custom and is entirely discretionary. Nobody's livelihood depends on tips. It is not customary to tip taxi drivers, porters at airports, or hairdressers, although you may do so if you wish. Porters have set charges at railway terminals, but not at hotels. Hotels and restaurants do not add service charges to accounts. In better-class restaurants, patrons sometimes tip food and drink waiters up to 10% of the bill, but only if service is good (if you are ecstatic about the service, make it 15%!) Tipping is exactly what it should be—an optional gratuity for good service. It has not developed into a means of subsidizing wages. If service is poor or a waiter is surly, don't tip.

TOILETS

Australians manage without euphemisms for "toilet," though in a country so rich in slang you won't be surprised to come across some wry synonyms. "Dunny" is the Outback slang term, but "washroom," "restrooms," "ladies," or "gents" are all understood. In Sydney, public toilets are often locked after certain hours, but you can generally use the facilities in any pub or cinema without making a purchase. Toilets are generally clean, even in the Outback. Sydney's most ornate toilets are located on the ground floor of the State Theatre on Market Street.

TOURIST INFORMATION OFFICES

The head office of the Australian Tourist Commission (ATC) is at Level 4, 80 William Street, Woolloomooloo, Sydney, NSW 2011; tel: (02) 9360-1111, fax: (02) 9331-2538.

Overseas ATC offices are

Hong Kong: Central Plaza, Suite 1501, 18 Harbour Road, Wanchai, Hong Kong; Tel. 802-7700; fax 802-8211.

Japan: Australian Business Centre, New Otani Garden Court Building, 28F 4-1, Kioi-cho, Chiyoda-Ku Tokyo, 102; Tel. (3) 5214-0720; fax (3) 5214-0719.

Korea: Suite 801, Hotel President 188-3, Ulchiro 1-ka, Chung-ku, Seoul 100-191; Tel. (02)779-8928; fax (02)779-8929.

New Zealand: Level 13, 44-48 Emily Place, Auckland 1; Tel. (09) 379-9594; fax (09) 307-3117.

Singapore: #17-03, United Square, 101 Thomson Road, Singapore 307591; Tel. 255-4555; fax 253-8431.

Taiwan: Trans-World Tourism Resources Inc, Suite 2208, 22nd Floor, World Trade Center, 33 Keelung Road, Section 1, Taipei; Tel. (2) 757-7188; fax (2) 757-6483.

United Kingdom: Gemini House, 10-18 Putney Hill, Putney, London SW15 6AA; Tel. (0181) 780-2229; fax (0181) 780-1496.

US: 2049 Century Park East, Suite 1920, Los Angeles CA, 90067; Tel. (310) 229-4870; fax (310) 552-1215.

The ATC employs travel counselors to answer questions about Australia. In Australia, the counselors can help arrange your itinerary or find a particular type of special-interest tour. The counselors can be e-mailed in advance from anywhere in the world using an electronic form available at the ATC web site: http://www.aussie.net.au. A reply is generally received within 24–48 hours.

Once in Australia, even in the smallest town you'll find outlet distributing local tourist information and advice free of charge. Look for the international "I" sign.

WEIGHTS and MEASURES

Australia uses the metric system of weights and measures. Speed and distance are measured in kilometers, goods in kilograms and liters, temperature in Celsius (Centigrade).

Sydney

Length

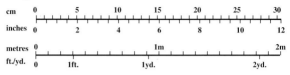

Weight

Temperature

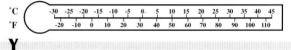

YOUTH HOSTELS

There are two types of hostel accommodations: privately owned back-packer hostels and YHA Hostels (Youth Hostels Association). Both provide self-catering accommodations from about A$20 a night. The Australian YHA is Australia's largest budget accommodation networks, running more than 130 hostels in just about every place you might want to go in Australia. "Youth" is a comparative term, as the hostels are open to all ages and offer sleeping areas, self-catering kitchens, and common rooms where you'll meet fellow travelers. You can join YHA in your own country or in Australia. Contact the YHA for a free information pack giving membership details and a list of hostels—422 Kent Street, Sydney, NSW 2001; Tel. (02) 9261-1111; fax (02) 9261-1969.

Sydney's Y on the Park Hotel is technically a YWCA, but you do not need to be young, a woman, or Christian to stay there. It's safe, comfortable, pleasant, very centrally located, and a very good deal. Normal YMCA/YWCA rules apply.

Recommended Hotels

Choosing a hotel in a city you're not familiar with can be daunting. Below is a selection of tried and trusted hotels to get you started. Sydney has a wide range of accommodations, everything from elegant five-star hotels with impeccable service to self-contained apartment hotels to hostels (see ACCOMMODATIONS on page 106 and TOURIST INFORMATION OFFICES on page 126). Most major international chains are represented. The pre-Olympics building boom has resulted in a fall in the average prices being charged by deluxe hotels and analysts expect this to persist at least until the immediate run-up to the Summer Olympics in September 2000.

The hotels in the following list are arranged in alphabetical order by location. Rates fall sharply once you move inland from the harborside neighborhoods.

The symbols below are a guide to the price of a standard double room with bath, excluding taxes and tips. Unless otherwise indicated, breakfast is not included. Prices are based on double occupancy on a midweek night. Many hotels in Sydney offer weekend discounts (of up to 30%); be sure to ask when making reservations. Downtown hotels are subject to a 10% bed tax.

❀❀❀❀	above A$250
❀❀❀	A$170–A$250
❀❀	A$100–A$170
❀	below A$100

The Rocks and Circular Quay

ANA Hotel Sydney ❀❀❀❀ *176 Cumberland Street, the Rocks, NSW 2000; Tel. (02) 9250-6000; fax (02) 9250-6250.* All rooms have harbor views and feature luxurious marble bathrooms. The rooms are spacious and the standards of service excellent. The bar has celebrated city views. Wheelchair access. 613 rooms. Major credit cards.

Hotel Inter-Continental Sydney ✪✪✪✪ *117 Macquarie Street, NSW 2000; Tel. (02) 9230-0200; fax (02) 9240-1240.* In an elegant building that incorporates Sydney's historic Treasury Building, the Inter-Continental combines 19th-century grace with 20th-century comfort. On one of the city's stateliest thoroughfares and within walking distance of the harbor, the Opera House, and the Royal Botanic Gardens. Swimming pool, health club, sauna, non-smoking floors. Pierpont's Bar stocks Australia's finest collection of Havana cigars. Wheelchair access. 497 rooms. Major credit cards.

Observatory Hotel ✪✪✪✪ *89–113 Kent Street, Millers Point, NSW 2000; Tel. (02) 9256-2222; fax (02) 9256-2233.* Smallish by the standards of five-star establishments but grand and elegant, with a serene grace that suggests the hotel has been welcoming guests for decades. In fact, it was built in the 1990s. A huge heated indoor pool and many other sumptuous amenities. On a quiet street within easy walking distance of the Rocks. Wheelchair access. 100 rooms. Major credit cards.

Old Sydney Parkroyal ✪✪✪✪ *55 George Street, NSW 2000; Tel. (02) 9252-0524; fax (02) 9251-2093.* Great location, with rooftop heated swimming pool, sauna, spa, and secure undercover parking. Wheelchair access. 174 guest rooms. Major credit cards.

Park Hyatt Sydney ✪✪✪✪ *7 Hickson Road, the Rocks, NSW 2000; Tel. (02) 9241-1234; fax (02) 9256-1555.* When it comes to location and facilities, this low-rise property is hard to beat. Press a button and the curtains slide open, revealing a view of the Opera House and sailing ships. A rooftop jacuzzi helps you slip into that holiday feeling. Popular with visiting celebrities. Wheelchair access. 158 rooms. Major credit cards.

Quay Grand ✺✺✺✺ *61–69 Macquarie Street, NSW 2000; Tel. (02) 9256-4000; fax (02) 9256-4040.* This all-suite "contemporary Art-Deco" hotel opened in March 1999 and offers uninterrupted views of Sydney Harbour, the Rocks, the Harbour Bridge, the city, and the Royal Botanical Gardens. You can watch Sydney's ferryboats from the main bar. Wheelchair access. 50 rooms. Major credit cards.

Regent Sydney ✺✺✺✺ *199 George Street, NSW 2000; Tel. (02) 9238-0000; fax (02) 9251-2851.* One of Sydney's original five-star hotels, the Regent has established a superlative reputation. Built in the 1980s, it closed for three months in 1999 to enlarge rooms and renovate. Personal service is great, the hotel is close to the harbor, and the dining room is renowned. Wheelchair access. 531 rooms. Major credit cards.

Ritz-Carlton Sydney ✺✺✺✺ *93 Macquarie Street, NSW 2000; Tel. (02) 9252-4600; fax (02) 9252-4286.* Opposite the Royal Botanical Gardens and filled with oil paintings, Persian rugs, and similar clubby trappings. At first the style proved too formal for laid-back Sydney, but the hotel has now got its act together. Wheelchair access. 106 rooms. Major credit cards.

Sydney Renaissance ✺✺✺✺ *30 Pitt Street, NSW 2000; Tel. (02) 9259-7000; fax: (02) 9251-1122.* Now owned by Marriott International, this hotel is close to the Stock Exchange and the Circular Quay ferry terminal. Floor-to-ceiling shutters make it possible to shut daylight out of the rooms entirely. Guests are supplied with their own hotel e-mail addresses at check-in. Wheelchair access. 579 rooms. Major credit cards.

City Center

All Seasons Premier Menzies Hotel ✺✺✺✺ *14 Carrington Street, NSW 2000; Tel. (02) 9299-1000; fax (02) 9290-3819.* One of Sydney's older hotels, the clubby Menzies has a traditional feel, but its spacious rooms, recently renovated, are outfitted with all the latest amenities. In the heart of Sydney's downtown area. Wheelchair access. 446 rooms. Major credit cards.

Hyde Park Plaza ❀❀❀ *38 College Street, NSW 2000; Tel. (02) 9331-6933; fax (02) 9331-6022.* Overlooking the park, this hotel offers a variety of self-contained apartments, ranging from studios to two-bedroom family suites and three-bedroom executive suites. Rates include a light breakfast in bed. The Hydeaway Cocktail Bar is a pleasant lounge for coffee and drinks. Wheelchair access. 182 rooms. Major credit cards.

Mercure Hotel Sydney ❀❀❀ *818–820 George Street, NSW 2000; Tel. (02) 9217-6666; fax (02) 9217-6888.* On Railway Square, within walking distance of Chinatown and Sydney's major entertainment venues. Sydney Football Stadium and Cricket Ground are also just minutes from the hotel. Wheelchair access. 517 rooms. Major credit cards.

Sheraton on the Park ❀❀❀❀ *161 Elizabeth Street, NSW 2000;Tel. (02) 9286-6000; fax (02) 9286-6686.* No harbor views, but you can gaze out on the verdant foliage of Hyde Park. The grand lobby and sweeping staircases are complimented by a sleek, modern health club and gym. Conveniently near Sydney's prime shopping venues and department stores. Wheelchair access. 559 rooms. Major credit cards.

Sydney Central YHA ❀ *Pitt Street and Rawson Pl., NSW 2000; Tel. (02) 9281-9111; fax (02) 9281-9199.* The winner of the 1998 Australian Tourism Award for Budget Accommodation. Technically a youth hostel, it's also an excellent, centrally located hotel in a heritage building opposite Central Station. A twin-share room with private facilities cost A$33 per person per night in 1999. Wheelchair access. 144 rooms. Major credit cards.

Sydney Hilton ❀❀❀❀ *259 Pitt Street, NSW 2000; Tel. (02) 9266-2000; fax (02) 9265-6065.* In a 43-story building (built 1975) with rooms beginning on the 20th floor, this Hilton

International–affiliated property offers the standard Hilton amenities. The stylish lobby is far classier than the building's exterior suggests. The Marble Bar downstairs is a Sydney institution. Wheelchair access. 585 rooms. Major credit cards.

Sydney Marriott Hotel ✹✹✹✹ *36 College Street, NSW 2010; Tel. (02) 9361-8400; fax (02) 9361-8599.* This hotel overlooks Hyde Park, not far from the Australian Museum. Rooms have abundant amenities—three telephones, remote control TV, individual climate control, iron and ironing board, microwave oven, tea and coffee makers, bathrobes, and hairdryer. Spa baths are available. Wheelchair access. 241 rooms. Major credit cards.

2 Bond Street ✹✹✹✹ *2 Bond Street, NSW 2000; Tel.(02) 9250-9555; fax 02) 9250-9556.* Studio apartments here include kitchens and cozy sitting rooms away from the sleeping areas. Centrally located, it's close to Sydney's financial district and within walking distance of Circular Quay. Wheelchair access. 185 rooms. Major credit cards.

The Wentworth ✹✹✹✹ *61–101 Phillip Street, NSW 2000; Tel. (02) 9230-0700; fax: (02) 9227-9133.* The Wentworth, a Rydges Hotel, has long been regarded as one of Sydney's grander establishments. Located in the heart of the CBD, the Wentworth is close to the Opera House, Circular Quay, the Rocks, and the Royal Botanic Gardens. 431 rooms. Major credit cards.

Darling Harbour

Grand Mercure Apartments ✹✹✹✹ *50 Murray Street, Pyrmont, NSW 2009; Tel. (02) 9563-6666; fax (02) 9563-6699.* Stylish two and three-bedroom apartments with private balconies, full kitchen, and laundry. Recreation facilities include indoor rooftop 25-m (80-ft) lap pool, spa, gym, and sauna. Within walking distance of Sydney Star Casino, Darling Harbour, and Cockle Bay Wharf. Wheelchair access. 121 rooms. Major credit cards.

Hotel Ibis Darling Harbour ✿✿–✿✿✿ *70 Murray Street, Pyrmont NSW 2009; Tel. (02) 9563-0888; fax (02) 9563-0899.* A quick walk from the attractions of Darling Harbour and Cockle Bay Wharf, and the Sydney Light Rail and Monorail trains stop at the hotel door. Easy access to Star City Casino, city-center shopping and entertainment, Chinatown, and Central Station. Wheelchair access. 256 rooms. Major credit cards.

Hotel Nikko ✿✿✿✿ *161 Sussex Street, NSW 2000; Tel. (02) 9299-1231; fax (02) 9299-3340.* Australia's largest hotel—its elegant, curved shape facing Darling Harbour belies its size. The Nikko is a short walk or monorail ride from the CBD and Sydney entertainment venues. Its Dundee Arms Pub is a pleasant watering hole. Wheelchair access. 645 rooms. Major credit cards.

Mercure Hotel Lawson ✿✿✿ *383–389 Bulwara Road, Ultimo, NSW 2007; Tel. (02) 9211-1499; fax (02) 9281-3764.* Located behind Darling Harbour within walking distance of the Powerhouse Museum and the Sydney Entertainment Centre, the Mercure provides friendly service. The great buffet lunch and refurbished conference center make this a popular convention venue. Wheelchair access. 96 rooms. Major credit cards.

Novotel Sydney on Darling Harbour ✿✿✿–✿✿✿✿ *100 Murray Street, Pyrmont, NSW 2009; Tel. (02) 9934-0000; fax (02) 9934-0099.* Overlooking the city skyline from Darling Harbour, the hotel completed a A$6-million refurbishment of all rooms in 1999. Guest facilities include full-size tennis court, outdoor pool, gym, and sauna. Wheelchair access. 527 rooms. Major credit cards.

East of City Center

City Crown Lodge ✿ *289 Crown Street, Surry Hills, NSW 2010; Tel. (02) 9331-2433; fax (02) 9360-7760.* Trim, pleasant property in a trendy street in inner-city Surry Hills, a short stroll from Oxford Street. Plenty of cafés and restaurants around.

Totally refurbished in 1997; all rooms have their own bathroom and balcony. 29 rooms. Major credit cards.

Furama Hotel Central ❀❀ *28 Albion Street, Surry Hills; Tel. (02) 9281-0333; fax (02) 9281-0222.* This pleasant new property close to Central Station offers clean, spacious accommodations just a short stroll away from Oxford Street and Chinatown. Wheelchair access. 270 rooms. Major credit cards.

Gazebo Hotel ❀❀❀ *2 Elizabeth Bay Rd. Elizabeth Bay, NSW 2011; Tel. (02) 9358-1999; fax (02) 9356-2951.* Great views of the harbor, the eastern suburbs, or the city skyline from most rooms. The Windows over Sydney rooftop restaurant and bar is a pleasant space to relax. Close to the Kings Cross nightlife and restaurant precinct. Wheelchair access. 384 rooms. Major credit cards.

Manhattan Park Inn ❀❀ *6–8 Greenknowe Avenue, Elizabeth Bay, NSW 2011; Tel. (02) 9358-1288; fax (02) 9357-3696.* Good value Art Deco–style property with sea views, built in 1926 and fully renovated in the mid 1990s. About 250 m from Kings Cross Station and 2 km (about a mile) from The Rocks. One room fully wheelchair equipped. 139 rooms. Major credit cards.

Medusa ❀❀❀ *267 Darlinghurst Rd., Darlinghurst, NSW 2010; Tel. (02) 9331-1000; fax: (02) 9380-6901.* A fine example of one of Sydney's new boutique hotels, Medusa offers 18 individually designed studios complete with stereo equipment, TV, microwave, and mini-kitchen. Bold light colors and huge beds. Attentive staff. The reflection pool in the courtyard is delightful. 18 rooms. Major credit cards.

Oxford Koala Hotel and Apartments ❀❀ *55 Oxford Street, Darlinghurst, NSW 2010; Tel. (02) 9269-0645; fax (02) 9283-2741.* Close to Hyde Park and the city center, this large hotel is on the route of Sydney's famous Gay and Lesbian Mardi Gras parade. Rooftop pool, parking, and a restaurant. Wheelchair access. 330 rooms. Major credit cards.

Ritz-Carlton Double Bay ❋❋❋❋ *33 Cross Street, Double Bay, NSW 2028; Tel. (02) 9362-4455; fax (02) 9362-4744.* Situated in leafy and pleasant Double Bay, a posh residential suburb, this inviting luxury property is just two blocks from the harbor. Stunning views from the rooftop pool, and plenty of restaurants nearby. Wheelchair access. 106 rooms. Major credit cards.

Sebel of Sydney ❋❋❋–❋❋❋❋ *23 Elizabeth Bay Road, Elizabeth Bay, NSW 2011; Tel. (02) 9358-3244; fax (02) 9357-1926.* The oldest five-star hotel in Sydney, this quiet and discreet hotel near Kings Cross tends to attract music and theater stars. The service is legendary; so is the cocktail bar, draped with signed photos of stars, some faded. Wheelchair access. 165 rooms. Major credit cards.

King Cross

Holiday Inn ❋❋❋ *203 Victoria Street, Potts Point, NSW 2011; Tel. (02) 9368-4000; fax: (02) 9267-4119.* Well positioned to catch the action in the Kings Cross precinct or nearby Oxford Street. The neighborhood is busy day and night, but the rooms are quiet and well appointed, with striking views across the city. Kings Cross underground station is close by. Wheelchair access. 278 rooms. Major credit cards.

New Hampshire Apartments ❋❋❋ *2 Springfield Avenue, Potts Point, NSW 2011; Tel. (02) 9356-3222; fax (02) 9357-2296.* Referred to affectionately by entertainers as the "Hamster," this hotel is in the lively Kings Cross nightlife and dining area. A gallery of fame in the lobby displays signed photos of visiting rock bands. One- and two-bedroom apartments are light and spacious and have wide harbor views. Wheelchair access. 54 rooms. Major credit cards.

Regent's Court Hotel ❋❋❋ *18 Springfield Avenue, Potts Point, NSW 2011; Tel. (02) 9358-1533; fax (02) 9358-1833.* A charming boutique hotel featuring suites with well-stocked kitchens. The building dates back to the 1920s, and the hotel kept to the spirit of that era in a stylish renovation. 29 rooms. Major credit cards.

North Sydney

Duxton Hotel North Sydney ❋❋❋–❋❋❋❋ *88 Alfred Street, Milsons Point, NSW 2061; Tel. (02) 9955-1111; fax (02) 9955-3522.* Long a favorite with corporate travelers, this hotel looks out across the harbor from a North Shore perspective, with views of the Harbour Bridge, the Opera House, and Centrepoint Tower. Executive suites, with fax and modem connections in all rooms, take up the top six floors. Wheelchair access. 165 rooms. Major credit cards.

Rydges North Sydney ❋❋❋ *54 McLaren Street, NSW 2060; Tel. (02) 9922-1311; fax: (02) 9922-4939.* Well-appointed rooms and self-contained suites are complemented by views of harbor and parks from private balconies. North Sydney, close to the city's commercial and shopping hub, is known for its pleasant gardens. Wheelchair access. 167 rooms. Major credit cards.

Bondi

Swiss-Grand Hotel Bondi Beach ❋❋❋ *Campbell Parade (corner of Beach Road), Bondi Beach, NSW 2026; Tel. (02) 9365-5666; fax: (02) 9130-3545.* Located right next to Bondi Beach, yet downtown Sydney and the airport are only 15–20 minutes away. Daily live entertainment in the lobby bar. Wheelchair access. 203 rooms. Major credit cards.

Manly

Radisson Kestrel Hotel ❋❋❋ *8–13 South Steyne, Manly Beach NSW 2095; Tel. (02) 9977-8866; fax (02) 9977-8209.* Manly is a 25-minute ride by Jetcat ferry from Circular Quay, but feels much further away. The property enjoys a pleasant beachside location and pleasant, comfortable rooms. Dinner on the balcony of the Sorrel Restaurant is a pleasant diversion. Wheelchair access. 83 rooms. Major credit cards.

Recommended Restaurants

Sydney restaurants flit into fashion, often to vanish within a few months of opening day. Sometimes the chef departs in a huff, other times the restaurant's demise remains a mystery. Despite this tendency, numerous restaurants have stood the test of time and established deservedly fine reputations.

The restaurants listed below are arranged alphabetically by location. Prices quoted are per person for a three-course meal excluding drinks and tip.

It is always advisable to phone ahead for a reservation, especially in high season.

❂❂❂	above A$50
❂❂	A$25–A$50
❂	below A$25

The Rocks and Circular Quay

Bennelong ❂❂❂ *137 Sydney Opera House, Bennelong Point, Tel. (02) 9250-7548.* Imaginative modern Australian menu in an acclaimed setting. The prime harborside setting is hard to beat. Major credit cards.

MCA Fish Café ❂❂❂ *140 George Street, Tel. (02) 9241-4253.* Try to get a table on the balcony—the views are sensational. The fish served here is super-fresh and succulent, line-caught rather than netted. Major credit cards.

Merrony's ❂❂❂ *2 Albert Street, Tel. (02) 9247-9323.* Modern Australian cooking with more than a hint of France. Smart, pleasant, and close to the harborside action. Major credit cards.

Rockpool ❂❂❂ *107 George Street, Tel. (02)9252-1888.* For ten years one of Sydney's most fashionable eateries, Rockpool serves innovative modern Australian cuisine in a stylish setting. Seafood excels. Major credit cards.

Sailor's Thai Canteen ❀❀ *106 George Street, Tel. (02) 9251-2466*. This isn't a canteen, nor is it frequented (particularly) by sailors—it's located in a former sailors' home and serves Thai food. For top views, try for a table on the balcony. Major credit cards.

The Wharf Restaurant ❀❀❀ *Pier 4, Hickson Road, Walsh Bay, Tel. (02) 9250-1761*. Not far from the Harbour Bridge, Pier 4 is known for its arts and theater. Fine harbor views, good modern Australian cooking, fashionable/artsy clientele. Major credit cards.

Downtown

BBQ King ❀ *18–20 Goulburn Street, Tel. (02) 9267-2433*. One of Chinatown's longest-running establishments. Fast service, bustling waiters, great food. Major credit cards.

Beppi's ❀❀❀ *Corner of Yurong and Stanley Streets, Tel. (02) 9360-4391*. One of Sydney's finest Italian restaurants, Beppi's has been in business since the 1950s. The wine list favors Italy and New South Wales. Major credit cards.

Bill and Toni ❀ *74 Stanley Street, East Sydney, Tel. (02) 9360-4702*. Lively and fun Italian family favorite. Generous helpings of pasta, mealballs, osso bucco, and other standards, plus free fruit drinks for the kids. Great coffee and sambucca downstairs. No credit cards.

Capitan Torres ❀❀ *73 Liverpool Street, Tel. (02) 9264-5574*. Set in Sydney's fledgling Spanish quarter (all two blocks of it), the Capitan serves hearty Spanish cuisine and jugs of hot-blooded sangria. Major credit cards.

Emperor's Garden ❀ *213 Thomas Street, Haymarket, Tel. (02) 9281-9899*. Fast and famous Cantonese cafeteria with speedy service and quality food at budget prices. Major credit cards.

Hyde Park Barracks Café ❀❀ *Queens Square, Macquarie Street, Tel. (02) 9223-1155*. Sydney restaurant locations don't come more historic than this former convict barracks. Prisoners survived on porridge, bread, and water; lunch these days is vastly more tempting. Major credit cards.

Johnnie Walker's Angus Restaurant ❋❋–❋❋❋ *25 Bligh Street, Tel. (02) 9232-6099*. Premier steak and seafood restaurant serving fine food and choice wines in traditional Australian surroundings. Popular since 1954, Johnnie Walker's has no need to be trendy. American Express, Visa only.

Darling Harbour

Ampersand ❋❋❋ *The Roof Terrace, Cockle Bay Wharf, Tel. (02) 9264-6666*. Two premier Sydney restaurateurs join forces in this top-of-the-range Japanese/French eatery set in rooftop gardens overlooking Darling Harbour. Major credit cards.

Potts Point

The Pig and the Olive ❋❋ *71A Macleay Street, Tel. (02) 9357-3745*. Noisy, bustling and fun, with great gourmet pizzas and Mediterranean-inspired dishes. Major credit cards.

Kings Cross and Darlinghurst

Balkan Seafood ❋❋ *215 Oxford Street, Tel. (02) 9331-7670*. Most of the delicacies grilling in the window are from the sea, but carnivores can enjoy Balkan specialties like *pola pola*. Given the right wind, the aroma of cooking carries a block. No credit cards.

Bayswater Brasserie ❋❋❋ *32 Bayswater Rd., Kings Cross, Tel. (02) 9357-2177*. Smart and stylish restaurant in the heart of Kings Cross. The clientele is often intriguing, and so is the imaginative Mod Oz cuisine. Major credit cards.

Oh! Calcutta! ❋ *251 Victoria Street, Tel. (02) 9360-3650*. The emphasis is on modern Indian food, but the menu includes dishes from Pakistan and Afghanistan as well. Stir-fried kangaroo with sesame seeds recently hopped onto the menu. Major credit cards.

Una's Café Restaurant ❋ *340 Victoria Street, Tel. (02) 9360-6885*. Traditional German and Austrian fare, from paprika

Schnitzel with potato Rösti to Sauerkraut and Kasseler Rippchen. No credit cards.

Surry Hills

The Dolphin Hotel ✹✹ *412 Crown Street, Tel. (02) 9331-4800.* Imaginative modern Australian cuisine served in a restaurant within a pleasant, newly refurbished pub. Sleek, stylish, friendly. Major credit cards.

Erciyes ✹ *409 Cleveland Street, Tel. (02) 9319-1309.* Cheap, cheerful, and well-patronized Turkish restaurant specializing in *pide* (Turkish pizza). Bellydancers perform most Friday and Saturday nights. Cash preferred; credit card identification necessary for checks over A$60.

Matsuri ✹ *614 Crown Street, Tel. (02) 9690-1336.* Lively establishment with unassuming décor and fast service. Proof that contemporary Japanese dining need not be expensive in Sydney. Major credit cards.

Mohr Fish ✹ *202 Devonshire Street, Tel. (02) 9318-1326.* An enticing variety of fresh fish and accompaniments. No reservations, but you can wait in the Shakespeare pub next door until a table clears. No credit cards.

Prasit's Northside on Crown ✹✹ *413 Crown Street, Tel. (02) 9319-0748.* Spicy Thai favorites served at high speed in a bustling, hip setting. There's another branch in North Sydney (Tel. (02) 9957-2271). Visa, Mastercard only.

Glebe

Darling Mills ✹✹✹ *134 Glebe Point Road, Tel. (02) 9660-5666.* Fine dining in capacious old sandstone surroundings in this artsy suburb. Modern Australian cuisine. Major credit cards.

Mixing Pot ✹✹ *178 St. John's Road, Tel. (02) 9660-7449.* Friendly Northern Italian establishment run by the same family for 18 years. Busy and cozy, with loads of atmosphere. Major credit cards.

Newtown

African Feeling ✹ *501 King Street, Tel. (02) 9516-3130.* Selected delicacies derived from several African cuisines served in pleasant surroundings on cosmopolitan King Street. The proprietors are from Nigeria. Major credit cards.

Old Saigon ✹ *107 King Street, Newtown, Tel. (02) 9519-5931.* Founded by renowned American Vietnam War correspondent Carl Robinson and his Vietnamese wife Kim, Old Saigon serves traditional Vietnamese fare. Carl has sold the establishment to his wife's family but still makes the occasional appearance. Major credit cards.

The North Shore

Bombay Heritage ✹✹ *82 Willoughby Road, Crows Nest, Tel. (02) 9906-5596.* Indian food with a difference. The Goan fish curry is renowned. Major credit cards.

Lavender Blue Café ✹✹ *165 Blues Point Road, McMahons Point, Tel. (02) 9955-7596.* Fun restaurant on the north side of the harbor, popular with business types, locals, and visitors. Modern Australian cuisine. Major credit cards.

The Red Centre ✹✹ *70 Alexander St., Crows Nest, Tel. (02) 9906-4408.* Mediterranean-inspired modern Australian cuisine with a touch of Asia in an Aboriginal-style setting. All of that plus pizzas. Major credit cards.

Thomas Street Café ✹✹ *2 Thomas Street, McMahons Point, Tel. (02) 9955-4703.* This hideaway garden café, well patronized by residents, offers seasonal modern Australian menus. A good place to relax and blend in with the locals. Major credit cards.

Inner Suburbs

Banjo Patterson Cottage ✹✹✹ *In the Park, Punt Road, Gladesville, Tel. (02) 9816-3611.* Well-prepared, high-quality modern Australian cuisine served in a historic sandstone cottage with sweeping views down the Gladesville River. Major credit cards.

Centennial Parklands ✿✿ *Inside Centennial Park (corner of Grand and Parkes Drives), Paddington, Tel. (02) 9360-3355.* Pleasant luncheon atmosphere in verdant surroundings; popular with families at play, especially on weekends. Innovative modern Australian cuisine. Major credit cards.

Minh ✿ *506 Marrickville Road, Dulwich Hill, Tel. (02) 9560-0465.* This cheerful, atmospheric Vietnamese restaurant branches into other Asian cuisines on its vast menu. Major credit cards.

Tetsuya's ✿✿✿ *729 Darling Road, Rozelle, Tel. (02) 9555-1017.* Fabulous flavors and masterful Japanese/French combinations distinguish this acclaimed gourmet favorite. Reservations are essential. Major credit cards.

Watson's Bay

Doyle's on the Beach ✿✿✿ *11 Marine Parade, Tel. (02) 9337-2007.* Founded in 1885, Doyle's has the best location for al fresco dining in Sydney. The seafood here is fresh and simple; the beachfront views are dazzling. Wear sunglasses. Visa, Mastercard only.

Bondi

Barzura ✿✿ *62 Carr Street, Coogee, Tel. (02) 9665-5546.* Modern Australian cooking, with influences ranging from Greek to Cajun. The appealing view across Coogee Beach, south of Bondi, adds extra sparkle. Major credit cards.

Raw Bar ✿✿ *35 Ramsgate Avenue, Bondi Beach, Tel. (02) 9365-7200.* Hip modern sushi bar popular with locals and visitors. Don't let the name fool you—it's not all raw. Major credit cards.

Sean's Panorama ✿✿✿ *270 Campbell Parade, Bondi Beach, Tel. (02) 9365-4924.* Always busy, and no wonder. Great modern Australian food served with verve within sight of Bondi's surf. You won't leave hungry. No credit cards.

ABOUT BERLITZ

In 1878 Professor Maximilian Berlitz had a revolutionary idea about making language learning accessible and enjoyable. One hundred and twenty years later these same principles are still successfully at work.

For language instruction, translation and interpretation services, cross-cultural training, study abroad programs, and an array of publishing products and additional services, visit any one of our more than 350 Berlitz Centers in over 40 countries.

Please consult your local telephone directory for the Berlitz Center nearest you or visit our web site at http://www.berlitz.com.

Helping the World Communicate